Also by Patricia Evans

The Verbally Abusive Relationship: How to Recognize It and How to Respond

Verbal Abuse Survivors Speak Out: On Relationship and Recovery

Controlling People: How to Recognize, Understand, and Deal with People Who Try to Control You

Teen Torment: Overcoming Verbal Abuse at Home and at School

THE VERBALLY ABUSIVE MAN *Can He Change?*

A Woman's Guide to Deciding Whether to Stay or Go

Patricia Evans

Adams Media

Avon, Massachusetts

Published by
Adams Media, an F+W Publications Company
57 Littlefield Street, Avon, MA 02322. U.S.A.
www.adamsmedia.com

ISBN 10: 1-59337-653-7
ISBN 13: 978-1-59337-653-6

Printed in the United States of America.

J I H

Library of Congress Cataloging-in-Publication Data
is available from publisher.

This publication is designed to provide accurate and authoritative
information with regard to the subject matter covered. It is sold with
the understanding that the publisher is not engaged in rendering
legal, accounting, or other professional advice. If legal advice or other
expert assistance is required, the services of a competent professional
person should be sought.
> —From a *Declaration of Principles* jointly adopted by a
> Committee of the American Bar Association and
> a Committee of Publishers and Associations

Many of the designations used by manufacturers and sellers to distin-
guish their product are claimed as trademarks. Where those designations appear in this book and Adams Media was aware of a trademark
claim, the designations have been printed with initial capital letters.

Notice: The author wishes to note that all women and men profiled in
this book are compilations. Unless otherwise noted, all identifying
characteristics have been changed.

*This book is available at quantity discounts for bulk purchases.
For information, please call 1-800-289-0963.*

ACKNOWLEDGMENTS

As if on a search for the Holy Grail, the cup, the ancient symbol of the feminine, people have searched for a solution to the most basic problem in relationships: control through verbal abuse. Without their questioning and questing, this book might not have been written.

My heartfelt thanks to all who so openly contributed to this work for sharing their thoughts, experiences, insights, and especially their questions.

Without the faith and encouragement of my publisher, Adams Media, this book would still be an idea in a folder. The entire staff has always been supportive. I especially thank Gary Krebs, enthusiastic, motivating, and managing it all; I thank my publicist Beth Gissinger for her dedication to bringing the message of this book to the world; Gene Molter, for moving publicity along with almost instant responses to my requests; and I am especially grateful to my editor, Jennifer Kushnier, whose valuable questions and painstaking devotion to detail refined the book you hold in your hands; and to Dr. William Higgins, who set the stage for this book with his direct and thoughtful foreword.

Thanks also to Christopher, Dorothy, Julie, Linda, Ron, and Stephanie for all their encouragement, and to my family for their enthusiastic support, especially to Lisa and Jennifer for their time in reviewing the manuscript.

—*Patricia Evans*

CONTENTS

FOREWORD

THE BASIC ASPECTS OF THIS book are significantly different from Ms. Evans's previous endeavors. Whereas her first book sought to define and describe the verbally abusive relationships between adults, this book delves deeper into the reasoning of both the perpetrator and the victim in relationships. It is part of her "style" to explain dynamics both from the woman's point of view and the man's point of view, striking a balance and not blaming either party for their inherent or learned relationship behaviors. Abusers, although predominantly male, may in some instances be female, and they define the victim's inner world as if they understand the victim's motives and thoughts, and believe on some level that they are the victim. This process culminates in an assault on and a loss of "self, mind, consciousness, and perception," rendering the victims convinced that they are to blame for the problems in their relationships, and causing them to feel "intrinsically flawed and unworthy."

Ms. Evans cites potential indicators of a willingness to change in the abuser, which include "reading, focused therapy, exercises, and anger management." Ms. Evans indicates most strongly that the only method for an abuser to change is if he can, and desires to. The impetus for this change takes the form of an agreement between the partners, presented by the victim.

Abusers, specifically verbal abusers, have discovered that anyone may impose their demands on another by becoming loud, insulting, dismissive, critical, threatening, or ultimately violent. In an effort to accommodate the abuser, the victim takes responsibility for the behaviors for which she's being blamed. Ultimately, a vicious cycle begins and the victim, if she attempts to seek help in the form of therapy, begins by blaming herself for all of the abuse perpetrated upon her. Since the children procreated in these relationships internalize the roles acted out by the fathers and mothers, the cycle of abuse is perpetuated.

From the standpoint of treatment, Ms. Evans states that the victim typically seeks help in an effort to either save or at least understand how she contributes to the dysfunction in the relationship. Whereas, typically, the psychotherapist attempts to empathize with the individual who enters therapy, this may become problematic when dealing with a verbally abusive relationship because then the victim becomes the "identified patient," which invariably implies that the victim, and not the perpetrator, is responsible for the dysfunction in the relationship. Conversely, Ms. Evans recommends that either the perpetrator participate in individual therapy, or that both parties participate in the therapeutic process without accusation or attribution of blame. The benefit of individual therapy for the abuser is that it provides the opportunity to address unconscious, internalized childhood beliefs that the abuser may possess, culminating in the self-perpetuating prophesy that he must be correct in his judgment.

This book, in many respects, breaks away from the articulation of the marital problems and focuses more on the rudimentary aspects of the issues and formulates appropriate treatment modalities.

In the realm of what we currently experience in the "family" court system, there are numerous flaws and inconsistencies. The current family court system is fraught with subjective opinions, abuses of power, and injustice. Individuals like Patricia Evans, in a straightforward manner, face the adversity of a dysfunctional system. If we all focused as much attention on remediation as Patricia Evans does, perhaps the children of divorce would not have to suffer the forfeit of the peace.

William L. Higgins, Ph.D.
Clinical and Forensic Psychologist
730 Evaluator for the State of California
Reunification Specialist

Innocent Words

Words mean nothing till you speak or pen them
Then they reveal the message in your heart
Words can bring joy and laughter
In song or prose
Words spoken and penned in poem
Can woo and romance grows
Yet innocent words uttered in anger and hate
Can cut like a knife and wound till it is too late
So choose unsuspecting words with wisdom and honor
For although your words, like an unfettered arrow,
May be forgotten
The piercing pain of words hitting another's heart
Is felt forever
We live in a yet unscripted world which our words have yet woven
So do not wield your words like a brandishing sword
But create a world of wonder with your well-spoken word

—Survivor of verbal abuse

Introduction

THE VERBAL ABUSER—
CAN HE CHANGE?

When I finished my fourth book, I thought that my readers had all the answers to their questions about verbal abuse. For example, they read that verbal abuse is much more than name-calling and that there are a dozen main categories of verbal abuse—from the silent treatment and discounting, to threats and name-calling. They read about other forms of control, coping, and recovery. They found out what goes on in the mind of the person who uses verbal abuse to control someone. Lastly, they saw how the controlling personality crystallized. They found ways to overcome verbal abuse at home and at school, how to talk to their own children, and how to reach out to young people.

The answers in these books, however, only led to more questions. Women called me saying, "I read all your books, but I want to know if you can tell me what to do to get him *to change*."

And this led to the question, "*Can* he change?" Over the years, I have been asked this question literally hundreds upon hundreds of times. It seems that it has become a burning question in the minds of thousands of women. They realize that they have been defined and denied their own experiences, as well as their right to empathy in a relationship.

I'm always glad to get notes and calls, but since my books simply led to more questions, the answers required another book—the book you hold in your hands.

In the following pages, I hope that you will find some answers to any questions you may have about whether a man who indulges in verbal abuse can change. I know that some men do change, but what are the possibilities for a particular man—perhaps the man in your own life—to do so? While no one can predict within anyone else the power to grow, integrate, and change that person's behavior, this book presents positive and negative indicators. Some indicators suggest that his changing is likely, and some point to the fact that his changing is highly unlikely. Of course, no one can change their behavior toward another person until they first realize, or wake up to, what they've been doing. Consequently, and most importantly, this book describes in detail the most effective way I have found to wake up the verbally abusive man (if, indeed, it is possible for him to wake up at all). At the same time, this way of waking him encourages him—even motivates him—to *want* to take the steps necessary to change.

If there is a possibility of his changing, I believe it is important to first know what is "wrong with him," then to utilize a strategy that could motivate him to do the work required to change. Whether you are reading this book to learn more about verbally abusive men, to help a friend, to counsel someone, or to see if your significant other will change, you will find helpful tools that hold the possibility of waking him up.

One of these tools is "the Agreement," which I describe in this book. In virtually all cases, no matter how many times the partner of a verbally abusive man may have told him what he was doing or how she felt, he either didn't get it or pretended that he didn't. Now, with the aid of "the Agreement," even *he* might see that he defines his partner—as if he knew her motives, knew her thoughts and what she was, and lived within her, as if he *were* her.

If the Agreement is going to be as effective as possible, it is important that anyone using it, or sharing its strategies with someone else, read and understand the preliminary information in the chapters leading up to Chapter 10 so that she will know what the possible outcome might be and how to present it to the abuser so that it has the most impact possible. No matter what the result, the person who presents the Agreement will know that she has done her very best to wake up the verbally abusive man to the fact that he has been defining his partner's inner world as if he did, indeed, live within her.

With this insight, he may begin the process of change—if he is willing. If he is not willing, then change will not be forthcoming. No one can make another person change. As I noted in my first book, *The Verbally Abusive Relationship*, there is nothing you can say or do to change another person; the other person must want to change for the sake of the relationship. The process of change involves reading, focused therapy, exercises, and effort. I suggest and explain such a plan in this book. If the verbally abusive man cannot begin taking the necessary steps to change, then he will not change. At the very least, if you present him with the Agreement and he refuses to accept or modify it appropriately, you will know that he cannot change.

At least you will know that about him.

Looking in the Mirror

Woe is me I'm undone
I've looked in the mirror
Seen what I've become
A verbal abuser, par none

Always covert and subversive as hell
When it's from the heart who needs to yell?
With just a scowl or sarcastic grin
My sullen anger was seething within

The venom of my words
The ones no one else heard
Brought sickness to her soul
And left her under my control

When she said, "I'm hurt"
I said it's no worse
Than the hurt I hurt
Thinking of me first
(Always thinking of me first)

God, what is this that I've done?
I invalidated, discounted, and made fun
When she wanted me to understand
I told her that I can't, I can't, I can't…

I traveled to the end of that road
And found that this reality showed
The things I had thought in my mind
To justify, to rationalize, to find
(A way to keep myself blind)

To the pain and hurt I caused
To heal would have cost
My reality and my pride
Of what I believed inside

"Crazy making" was the word
Always twisting what was heard
Never saying what was meant
The desire "to win" was evident

In every conversation we had
I was the good one she was the bad
I made sure I was the last one heard
Always needing to have the last word

Now you've shown me the price
Of my wife's constant sacrifice
The debt is so enormously great
I try to understand and appreciate

Only you can pay the cost
It's contained in your cross
I cry to you for forgiveness
Without you all is lost

—A verbally abusive man who has
woken up to what he has done

1

ABOUT CHANGE

THROUGHOUT THIS BOOK, I REFER to the person who consistently indulges in verbal abuse as "the abuser." This is not to judge or label that person, but to facilitate reading the book. Similarly, as this book is primarily a woman's guide to deciding whether her verbally abusive man can change, I refer to the abuser as male and his significant other—that is, the victim—as female; I call her "the partner." Having said this, if you, the reader, are experiencing verbal abuse from your mate and want him to change, it is very important that in all the interactions you have with him you not define him by saying, "You're a verbal abuser." A good rule of thumb is to always address his *behavior*, not label *him*. If you, as the partner, say, "That sounds like verbal abuse," you define his behavior but not him.

If you are wondering if your mate will change and whether you should stay or go, then helping him to recognize his behavior and knowing how to motivate him is essential. A key way to motivate a verbally abusive man to change is to awaken him to what he is doing and to do so in such a way that he realizes that he is acting irrationally and harmfully. Most importantly, he realizes that when he tells her what she is, he is, in a certain sense, *pretending to be her.* I have found that there is a way to motivate him to change, in the form of a mutual agreement—what I term "the Agreement." It shows the abuser what he is doing and why. Later chapters show how to prepare for it, write it, present it, and follow up after presenting it.

The strategies in this book, particularly the Agreement, hold the possibility of waking up the verbally abusive man—but *not* in all cases. Some men are unable or unwilling to recognize that they are verbally abusive and that this abuse is a symptom of a deeper problem. Generally speaking, however, until they become aware, they don't even think of themselves as irrational or abusive; I have found this to be true of all the men I have talked and consulted with. Instead, even when behaving abusively, many men feel that they are reacting with restraint to an actual attack by their partners. Some verbally abusive men can't change in the way they relate to their partners, and some, even when they do realize that they are behaving both irrationally and harmfully, don't want to put forth the effort that real change requires. This book reveals who is most likely and who is least likely to change. Further, it points out the clues that indicate change is taking place.[1]

WHEN THE VERBAL ABUSER IS A WOMAN

Some readers may be wondering why I don't ask, "The verbal abuser—can he *or she* change?" Women can certainly be controlling and abusive toward their mates, so why does this book focus just on men changing, especially when, in introducing the term "verbally abusive relationship" in 1992, I said that women could be the perpetrators?

Simply put, although I've seen men change, *I have never seen a woman transform from seriously verbally abusing her mate to treating him with empathy.* The therapists I've talked with about this issue have not seen verbally abusive women change either. I will not say that it would be impossible, because I cannot say anything is impossible when it comes to the human psyche, only that it is highly unlikely. Although I have been a consultant to many hundreds of women who were verbally abused, and also to some men who were likewise abused, most of the men who call me want to stop their own abusive and controlling behaviors. While thousands of women have told me stories of how they were verbally abused, only three women in a dozen years ever made appointments with me because they themselves were abusive—and all three cancelled at the last minute!

If you are reading this book, hoping your wife or female significant other will change; will stop telling you what you are, what you think, what you should do, what your opinions should be; or will stop raging at you when you explain yourself or when you ask nicely, "Please don't do that," or "Please don't call me that," you may try the strategies in this book, but please know that the odds are against your partner changing. I cannot tell you how she could change. I have yet to see a woman change from verbally abusing her mate to validating him (or her, as the case may be).

Why is it so unlikely she will change? Because for a woman to be abusive over time in her relationship, she must first lose her inner world, her feelings, her intuition, and her receptivity; she must be severed from all that the culture ascribes to the feminine, and so she must be very damaged, indeed. (The exception is the woman who has simply withdrawn from her mate who has been verbally abusive, unkind, uncaring, and not empathetic toward her.) Conversely, for a man to be abusive over time in a relationship with a woman, he need only conform to a culture—and sometimes a father, and occasionally also a mother—that severs him from his inner world, that says, more or less, "Real men don't cry," "Don't be a wimp," "Suck it up," "You're being a baby," or, "It's not happening."

THE NEED FOR CHANGE

After publishing four books on verbal abuse and control (see Appendix B, page 247), I have heard from thousands of women who say, in effect, "I know what verbal abuse is. I know it relates to control. I know what is going on, but, please, Patricia, can you tell me *how* to get my abuser to stop? No matter how many times I say, 'Stop,' or, 'That hurts,' he doesn't think he's doing anything wrong, or he thinks it's all my fault, or that it shouldn't bother me. Sometimes he just says, 'It didn't happen.'" Here are some other questions and comments I've heard:

- "How can I get him to see what he's doing?"
- "How can I tell if he's even capable of change?"
- "Can you tell me how I can tell if he's really changed?"
- "He knows he's been abusive. He knows he's hurt me, but then he goes back to his abusive ways saying it's my fault. It seems that he's locked into having power over me, locked into trying to control me, but at the same time, he doesn't see himself as controlling at all. Not only that, he doesn't seem to feel he's privileged or superior to me. Instead, he says he feels attacked." (Speaking of a man's reaction to an attack, I want to mention battering, a very overt form of abuse meant to control the partner; verbal abuse is a less overt form. Verbal abuse precedes all domestic

violence, although not all verbal abusers become physically abusive.)

- "One time we separated. He kept telling me he'd changed. But when we got back together, he hadn't. What is really hard for me to get my mind around is that when he told me he'd changed he actually seemed to think that he had."
- "I think he's changed. But how can I be sure the changes will last?"

Many men seem to have changed as soon as they are separated from their partners. The verbally abusive man cannot maintain a change from verbally abusive to validating behaviors, unless he knows what drives them. For change to last, he must wake up to the reality of his partner's experience and his own unconscious motives. This book presents a truly effective way to not only wake the verbally abusive man to his behavior but also to motivate him to do the work to change.

VERBAL ABUSE DEFINED

Verbal abuse defines people in some negative way, and it creates emotional pain and mental anguish when it occurs in a relationship. I invite you to take a peek at Appendix A, on page 227, for some common verbally abusive statements. Some are much more common than I ever thought. For instance, I had never heard "Shut your pie hole" until, during a consultation, a client happened to mention being ordered to silence this way. Curious, I asked a few callers later that day if they had ever heard the phrase. Actually, three out of four had heard it from the verbally abusive men in their lives. Though most of my clients are well educated, as are their spouses, what goes on in their homes behind closed doors would hardly be believed outside of a TV horror show.

Any statement that tells you what, who, or how you are, or what you think, feel, or want, is defining you and is, therefore, abusive. Such statements suggest an invasion of your very being, as if to say, "I've looked within you and now I'll tell you what you want, feel, etc." Similarly, threats are verbally abusive because, like torture, they attempt to limit your freedom to choose and thus to define yourself. Of course, if you have defined yourself to someone, "I'm Suzy's Mom," and that person says, "That's Suzy's Mom," they are affirming or validating what you have said. On the other hand, verbal abuse is a lie told to you or told to others about you. If you believe the lie, it would lead you to think that you are not who you are or that you are less than you are.

For instance, one of the most common ways a verbally abusive man abuses his partner is by telling her that she is "too sensitive." This behavior defines her inner reality and assaults her consciousness. "You're too sensitive" is a lie. "She blows things out of proportion" is another lie but one that is told to someone else. A woman who is told that she is too sensitive often tolerates increasing levels of verbal abuse because she is trying to show her loved one that she is *not* "too sensitive." Her life becomes paradoxical. The more she believes the abuser, the less sensitive she actually becomes, until what would be excruciatingly emotionally painful to anyone in such a relationship is so suppressed, she spaces out and does not feel it, or she feels it but does not remember what was said to her.

Another common way the abuser defines his partner is by walking away when she is asking a question, or mentioning something, or even in the middle of a conversation. By withholding a response, he defines her as nonexistent. (Such behaviors perpetrated by women are also verbally abusive, except when they are walking away from abuse and protecting themselves.)

Some defining statements, however, such as "You're so beautiful," are not abusive. This statement is understood to mean,

"From my perspective, you are really beautiful." But people don't usually speak in that way. Although it is a defining statement, it is understood to be a compliment or a positive stroke. Nevertheless, one of the most respectful ways of saying something positive is to say, for example, "Can you see how I see you as really beautiful?"

When women ask me, "Can he change?" they are talking about one kind of change in particular: change from verbally abusive to validating, respectful behaviors. In other words, they are asking about men's ability to change from defining to nondefining behavior. Defining statements are the opposite of affirmations, which are positive statements that confirm what we know and value about ourselves. For example, when a man says, "I hear you. I understand," even if he does not agree with you, he validates or confirms what you have expressed to him. If, however, he says, "You're too sensitive," or "Where did you get a crazy idea like that," he invalidates and defines you.

THE AGREEMENT

Change cannot even begin until the verbally abusive man gets his first wakeup call to what he is doing to his partner. This wakeup call is the Agreement. I will show you in detail how to formulate it so that it is clear, tailored specifically to your abuser's behavior, and designed to motivate change. The Agreement is founded upon the categories of verbal abuse that I discussed in depth in *The Verbally Abusive Relationship* (withholding, countering, discounting, verbal abuse disguised as jokes, blocking and diverting, accusing and blaming, judging and criticizing, trivializing, undermining, threatening, name calling, forgetting, ordering, denial, and abusive anger). Although the categories of verbal abuse give us an objective view of verbal abuse—for instance, "this is judging," or "that is ordering"—the Agreement organizes the basic kinds of abuse in a different way, according to what the abuser is telling his partner. For example, if the abuser says, "You're stupid," the partner might ask herself, "What is he telling me?" She might then say, "He is telling me what I am," rather than say, "That is name calling, a category of verbal abuse." For the ways to organize verbal abuse for use in the Agreement, turn to Appendix A, page 227.

The Agreement is further based on the model of the abuser's illusionary world, as I described in *Controlling People* and which I touch upon in Chapter 3. The abuser's illusions allow him to define his partner's inner world—how she should be, what she feels, and so forth—without feeling as though he has lost his mind or his capacity to reason. In fact, one of his illusions is that he knows her inner world just as if he were her.

If you are a therapist, counselor, partner of an abuser, student, helping professional, friend, or relative of either the perpetrator or the partner in a verbally abusive relationship, this book will shed light on the problem of verbal abuse. It will also show you what it takes for the verbally abusive man to wake to what he is doing and choose to be courageous enough and strong enough to stand on his own two feet and not in the body/mind/soul of his partner.

If you, as the abused partner, choose to see whether your husband, fiancé, or boyfriend will wake up, want to change, and take the steps to change, I will show you precisely how to form the Agreement and how best to present it so that it is heard and seen by the man who has verbally abused you. Since it is based in mutuality, I will also show you how either person can modify it, and how either person can respond to any infringements. With the presentation of this Agreement, many men who have indulged in verbal abuse during most of their relationship hear their partners for the first time. They actually get their first glimpse of what they've been doing for some time, be it weeks or decades. And some men do the work to change.

Many women are deeply concerned over such questions as: What is the likelihood of change? What does fake change look like? Are there any possible dangers in even asking for change? Will I have to be on guard and working at this constantly? What are the signs of change? Does presenting the Agreement to my mate mean I'm committed to staying in my relationship?

I will address these issues in coming chapters and offer some guidelines so that the partner of a man who indulges in verbal abuse can assess her situation, decide when and where to present the Agreement, and know how it can be valuable even if she doesn't plan to stay in her relationship.

I can't guarantee that the Agreement and other suggestions in this book will wake up the abuser and motivate him to change, but they might. They have certainly allowed some men to see for the first time that they were saying all kinds of irrational things, trying to silence and control the very people they thought were closest to them: their significant others, their spouses, and their children, sometimes even their employees and coworkers. Until they heard and saw the Agreement, many abusers had no idea that they were acting irrationally, nor did they know why.

By understanding their fears and what is behind their seemingly fearless façade, by choosing to be rational rather than irrational, men can begin taking the steps to change and, most importantly, to make their change permanent.

In the next chapter, I will explore the implications of verbal abuse—particularly the need for change. As I have noted, domestic violence begins with verbal abuse, and although all verbal abusers may not become physically violent, they certainly create pain and fear in their homes and very often impact their children. Eventually their children do not know what is normal and what is not. Children from abusive homes may learn not to feel, may learn to become perpetrators or victims, and may try to perfect themselves through eating disorders and compulsive behaviors or to escape in drugs and alcohol. Bottom line: Defining people and their inner world is a very irrational behavior. It is mind numbing and very scary to the recipient, especially when the person who is behaving irrationally says, "I love you."

2

THE VERBALLY ABUSIVE MAN AND DREAM WOMAN

SOME WOMEN HAVE TOLD ME that they were more concerned with feeling better than in knowing what was "wrong" with their spouses. But, somewhat paradoxically, the more the partner of a verbally abusive man knows what is going on with him, the more relieved she may be. Knowing what is behind a verbally abusive man's behavior renders it more obvious and more clearly his problem.

When I talk with my clients about their experiences and the bizarre verbally abusive comments they hear from their husbands or boyfriends, they often say that they just can't understand why he says the things he says. Some women feel as if they are going crazy. The abuse is inexplicable. The partner cannot imagine why he acts like he does. Understanding, but never accepting, his behavior can lead toward a cure and makes a great deal of sense. Understanding the sickness relieves some of the partner's struggle to be "good enough" or to prove to him that what is happening is not her fault.

Imagine you have a best friend in the entire world, that you and she have shared your hearts with each other since grammar school, and that one day a small piece of jewelry that is very precious to you is missing. Imagine searching and wondering what could have happened to it. Then a few weeks later, a small silver antique box is gone from the tabletop where you were sure you had left it. Later something else is missing, and slowly you come to the realization that these items disappeared when your friend came to visit. Can you imagine feeling devastated? How could this person betray you? What kind of friend would do that? You might think, "Do I have something wrong with me not to have seen it? To have a friend like that?" While you try to understand why she would do this, you find out through another friend that she is a diagnosed kleptomaniac. Suddenly you don't feel quite so betrayed and angry, but kind of sorry for her, even though you know you can no longer trust her alone in your home.

Discovering what is wrong with an abusive man is like discovering that this friend you know so well is suffering from kleptomania. When the partner of an abuser knows *why* her husband or boyfriend does what he does, she finds it much easier to let go of the blame heaped upon her. She may doubt herself, however, if, even when she believes that the abuse is not her fault, she hears an authority figure, parent, friend, counselor, or sibling, whose judgment she trusts, say, "try harder," or "love heals all things." If she is accused, "What did you do to provoke him?" or blamed, "He must have a reason for getting so angry," she may still believe that there must be something she could do to make the abuse stop. If she is told that the problem in the relationship rests with her, that she has somehow become a "codependent," she will spend another half dozen years trying to figure out what is wrong with her, that she has some malfunction that causes the problem, her own abuse, and her own pain. And maybe worst of all, if her spouse tells her that God expects her to stay in the relationships and to try harder, she may believe that this is true. It is important for her to know that she is hearing a lie. Her spouse has pretended to speak for God. And what does God say? Surprise! Just what her spouse says. If he tells her that the Bible backs him up, that too is a lie. (In Appendix D, page 253, I've listed books about the Bible and abuse from a Christian perspective.)

In order to see that it's not your fault, let's look at the verbally abusive man through a new lens. He shows distinct symptoms, but what is going on with him? He defines his partner. He has an angry demeanor at home or is very cold and unresponsive. He usually won't answer a direct question about himself. He rarely, if ever, asks his partner about herself: how she is feeling, what she likes, what bothers her about something. He seems not to really see her. He acts as if he has been assaulted when she tells him that she is unhappy about something. He counters her separate thoughts and opinions. He defines her in many ways, but seems not to realize it, rather like a man living in the United States in the 1850s who hears his wife say, "I'd like to vote in the next election." He thinks, *Is she crazy?* "You're not capable!" he says. Thus, he defines her.

There is a deeper reason why some men are verbally abusive, and there is a way to see why they are the way they are. Although some men joke about their "Other Half" when they speak of their partners, in a very real way, the partner *is*, from her abuser's perspective, his other half. Most verbally abusive men are not abusive simply because they feel that they are privileged or superior to their partner—although some do. And most verbal abusers don't think that they are trying to dominate and control their partners. Some even think their partners are trying to control them!

DREAM WOMAN

Most men who indulge in verbally abusive behavior do so because they feel attacked by their partners. When they feel attacked, they attack back. But why do they feel attacked by their partners in the first place? Because their real-life, flesh-and-blood partner, whom I call a real woman, shows up in the body where a dream woman was supposed to be.

Just what is the dream woman? Though I explain this syndrome in my third book, *Controlling People*, I'll briefly explain it here, as we can hardly discuss the verbally abusive man without discussing this hidden part of him. A dream woman is the personification of the abuser's unconscious, unintegrated self. For instance, if he wasn't allowed to cry when he was a little boy, and he was supposed to be so tough that he didn't complain if he was physically hurt, he had to block off his pain. He couldn't "know" what happened to him. He couldn't even use his feeling function to know what he was feeling, or his sensate function to know when he was hurt. A huge part of him became like a separate self within him. And this "separate self" became what I call the dream woman. She is composed not only of the experiences in his life that he didn't integrate, but also those qualities, functions, energies, talents, and even gifts that were left in his unconscious self, particularly those qualities *ascribed* to the feminine that he never developed. All this composes the dream woman. And, although he may have some dream children, even dream employees, Dream Woman can be thought of as mostly *the rest of him*.

The dream woman is not simply an imaginary ideal. When the abuser can't find his dream woman, he can't find *the rest of himself*. The dream woman accounts for most men's verbally abusive behavior and for its Jekyll and Hyde quality. The verbal abuser uses anger and abuse to shape and control his partner, to make her be his dream woman.

When the verbal abuser feels most secure—for instance, right after marriage—he anchors the dream woman in his partner. It is like he blows her up with his thoughts like a balloon doll. Then the real woman becomes a threat to him. Her existence can seem like an attack. The abuser is threatened by his partner's separateness from him. She is no longer an "extension" of himself. When his partner shows up, the verbally abusive man can't find his dream woman—the part of himself that lives within her. So much of him is now within his partner, that he can't find himself when the real woman appears, talking or walking differently from the dream woman. Possibly the real woman is talking about a new baby, the way that Laci Peterson must have, and thus, not as focused on him as his dream woman would be. Most of these men are trying to make their partners into dream women and become angry when they can't get the real woman to say or do what she is "supposed" to do at any given moment. To suddenly not find the rest of himself, to not find his inner world of feelings, sensations, and intuitions, his unlived unintegrated self, is to lose *that which connects him to reality itself.* After all, how do we know we are here? By the way we feel, sense, and intuit the world around us.

The abuser, being bonded to his dream woman instead of being bonded to himself, is bonded in the way that the nucleus of an atom is bonded with electrons and neutrons, bonded with such a powerful force that when it is broken there is an atomic explosion. When the abuser is bonded like that to his unlived self (his dream woman), to see the real woman is to see the bond broken, to feel the great rift between himself and all that (to him) makes him real here on planet Earth.

Men who indulge in a pattern of verbally abusive behavior aimed at their wives or girlfriends are actually attempting to keep a dream person (the dream woman) alive and well in her body. It is as if they were eradicating their real partner to shape her into their dream one. Albeit unconscious, their attempts to create a new being, a dream woman, are tantamount to placing themselves above God, the Divine, the First Source. While attempting to silence the real woman, the verbally abusive man is also trying to make her into "his" image and likeness, to resurrect his own creation, one that thinks what he thinks, wants what he wants, and always knows what he means. Playing God is dangerous. Hence, *his changing is essential.*

In the most extreme cases, the verbally abusive man is missing so much of himself, he might be seen as a psychological quadriplegic—missing much of his feeling, sensate, and intuitive functions, even his humanity. The dream woman is huge for him. She is composed of all that he is missing. When he can't find her, he feels severed from himself and, therefore, so attacked that he may severely batter, even kill, his partner (the real woman). This accounts for most domestic violence. If the violence becomes a homicide/suicide, it is likely because he has suddenly, by his own hand, lost the body that harbored his dream woman, and he does not want to go on without her.

Let's keep in mind that the verbally abusive man believes he is truly a fine person, and that he often truly believes anything he says is nothing compared to what his partner does to him. What does she do? She shows up and displaces his dream woman (the rest of himself).

Leaving a man this damaged can be dangerous for the partner. He might view losing control of the body that harbors his dream woman as a "killing attack" against himself. Killing the real woman, or committing a homicide/suicide could be the outcome. I believe that Nicole Simpson was the victim of such an attack. Her ex-husband, O.J., was found guilty of murder in a civil court in California. Why would O.J. have killed his ex-wife (if, in fact, he did)? From the dream-woman perspective, it could only be because he had never withdrawn his unlived self, his dream woman, from her. Just before the famous murder, O.J.

had attended his daughter's dance recital. There, he had seen his ex-wife Nicole, who reportedly told him he could not join her and her family for dinner. It appears that he actually thought his ex-wife would invite him to dine with her and her family after their daughter's recital, even though he had battered and abused her, stalked her, and terrified her.[2] According to reports, Nicole told him that he could not join her and her family for dinner after the recital. His dream woman would have said that he could. He could not deny Nicole's response because others were present. The real woman had appeared in the body where he had anchored his dream woman. Severed from himself, unable to find the rest of himself, might he have felt this separation to be a killing attack, prompting him to attack back? From another perspective, we might say that if O.J. hadn't had a dream woman anchored in Nicole, he would never have imagined that a woman who was terrified of him, whom he had battered and abused, would want to eat dinner with him.

HIS SEPARATE REALITY

When a man defines his partner, he does not see or hear her but rather, is in a different reality. I explain this "reality" in *The Verbally Abusive Relationship*. Let's look at this perspective. His reality, even if it seems quite crazy or at least very irrational, is about maintaining his dream woman and his own perfected persona, or image, to the world. And, it is about erasing the real woman. Therefore, it is about Power Over and control of his partner. Despite his controlling behavior, he may not see himself as controlling. Instead, he may simply feel attacked by his partner's separateness and believe that he is only responding to an attack. We know that he is not his partner. He is not a woman. He does not live within her. He does not know what she thinks, means, or is—not without asking, he doesn't. But he doesn't know that yet. Until he sees the Agreement, he does not yet know how often he pretends to be his partner and, consequently how often he pretends to be a woman.

In his world, making up what his partner is, thinks, feels, and so forth is perfectly rational, or at least okay. One way to see how the verbally abusive man can define his partner's inner world, with statements such as, "You're too sensitive," or "You're trying to start a fight," is to imagine that he has a movie reel running in his mind and his partner is the *main character.* In his movie, his partner (his dream woman) is saying and doing a particular thing at each moment, possibly like an "all-needs-meeting mother" or a "beauty queen" (depending on what movie is running in his mind). So when the real woman asks a question, brings up a topic for conversation, or tells him about something important to her, she shows her separateness and he feels attacked. It's as if a character in his movie looked out from the screen and struck up a conversation. It can't be happening! Unconsciously, she *is* his dream woman. And now his whole world (the movie) is falling apart. His world is being shattered! He has no control; he is losing the main character that is, incidentally, a part of himself. Losing this part of himself could feel like the greatest attack and rejection one could imagine.

A CONVERSATION WITH THE DREAM WOMAN

Since the husband or significant other who had indulged in verbal abuse is the very man who is going to converse with his partner as he works though his process of changing, it is valuable for him to understand what happens when his dream woman is part of the conversation. For this reason, we will look at "the picnic dialogue" so both parties can see what verbal abuse in communication looks like and how entrapped the partner can be when she attempts to explain or defend herself. In this example, she explains herself instead of repeating the question she asked him in the first place. If the partner does not repeat the question and instead tries to defend herself, then she faces a great deal of trauma.

I present the following typical scenario to illustrate the confusion and pain verbal abuse generates. Jack, the verbal abuser, is, metaphorically speaking, in a dream state, trying to thwart Jill, the real woman, so he can stay in his illusory state with his dream woman. It is an inescapable fact that his dream woman played an enormous role in the entire scenario. As is usual, she is behind the scenes. No one, not even Jack, the antagonist, knows she is there. The scene also illustrates what the partner might say and do to bring awareness to her mate.

A word of warning: If you have experienced verbal abuse, just reading the dialogue may trigger flashbacks or trauma, as happened to one woman, who wrote, "As I'm reading through your book, my head is spinning and my heart races itself to a level of anxiety that I only experienced when in those relationships. Even though they are just words on a page, they put me right back into the abuse." If you notice any of these symptoms as you read the picnic dialogue, please just go on to the next chapter.

To read this dialogue, I suggest that you first quickly read the lines that are underlined. They alternate between Jack and Jill so that you do not have to read their names to follow it. After reading the dialogue between angry Jack and struggling Jill, I suggest you go back and read the analysis in brackets. This way, Jill's confusion will show up most dramatically. After each interaction, I point out the category of verbal abuse that was used; these words appear in boldface type and in some way define the partner. (I discuss these categories in depth in *The Verbally Abusive Relationship*.) In the following scenario Jack diverts Jill from getting an answer by accusing her of insisting he have plans. He thus defines her intentions and the meaning of her words.

Jack and Jill Discuss the Picnic

Jack and Jill have been together for seventeen years. This scene took place about a year before Jill gave Jack "the Agreement." Their two children, a boy of fifteen and a girl of thirteen, are visiting cousins at a ranch out of town where they will stay for the weekend. Jack and Jill have a nice upper-middle-class home and a good bank account with no money problems. Jill works at a travel agency with some flex time; Jack works as a manager of the data analysis department of a large company. Their children are doing well in school, and their life, looking in from the outside, appears almost ideal.

We enter Jill and Jack's home. It is dusk. What's really going on here? Is this an argument or abuse? What are the dynamics?

Jack and Jill are relaxing in their home, looking at the television. During a break, the following conversation ensues *(read underscored dialogue first)*:

JILL: <u>Honey, I was wondering: Do you have any plans for tomorrow?</u> (A simple question, but Jill shows up as a separate person from Jack. She doesn't know his plans. His dream woman would, so he becomes angry.)

JACK *(fiercely)*: <u>What do you mean, "plans"?</u> [*Angrily:*] <u>Do I have to have plans?</u> (Jack **diverts** Jill with a question and **blocks** her by not answering yes or no, thereby avoiding responding to the real woman. He confabulates[3] a reason for his anger over losing his dream woman, **accusing** Jill of implying that he has to have plans. He is expressing **abusive anger**.)

JILL: <u>Well, no, I just thought it might be fun to go up to the mountain and take a picnic tomorrow since the kids won't be back until Sunday.</u> (Explaining is a trap in an abusive relationship. Jill notices Jack's question "what do you mean" and seems to sense his confusion and anger at her. She doesn't know about his dream woman, so she explains her reason for asking instead of simply repeating the question, "Do you have any plans for tomorrow?")

JACK: <u>Well, why didn't you just say so?</u> (Jack **blames** Jill for his anger and angrily reprimands her with another question. He still avoids answering the real woman's question because in no way will he respond to a real woman as if she is real.)

JILL: <u>I did, just now.</u> (She tries to answer Jack's second question. She is confused and is still trying to explain herself, thinking everything will be all right.)

JACK: <u>Oh come on, you know I can't stand it when you don't get to the point.</u> (Jack **counters** Jill, again **diverting** by changing the subject; he is **blaming** Jill for his own anger and **accusing** her of being indirect. In telling her what she knows and that she doesn't "get to the point," he is defining her. He once again confabulates a reason for his anger, since he doesn't know about his dream woman. He just can't find his dream woman so he feels attacked and adrift.)

JILL: <u>But, I did.</u> (Jill is now defending and explaining herself because of the accusation that she has done something that Jack can't stand. She has again been diverted from her original question, "Do you have any plans for tomorrow?")

JACK: <u>Would you just quit arguing? We'll go up to the mountain if that's what you want.</u> (Jack **accuses** Jill of arguing and makes her responsible for his agreeing to go on the picnic, as if he were reluctantly giving in to her. Actually, he is reluctant to answer and thereby acknowledge the real woman. He's angry because he had to answer the real woman, that is, lose his dream woman. And, telling her what she is doing, "arguing" is, of course, defining her.)

JILL: <u>Well, what do you want to do?</u> (Jill doesn't want him to feel forced to go, as she would consider other fun things to do. Asking what he wants to do is her only thought as a way to show him that she is not trying to argue or be the "bad guy." She is in pain and does not want to be blamed for her pain.)

JACK: <u>Didn't I just say we'll go? What more do you want?</u> (He implies she wants more from him, thus **accusing** her, defining her, and speaking in a condescending way. Actually, he is angry because it stressed him greatly to respond to the real woman.)

(Jill is looking distraught, almost sick. He seems mad. He doesn't really want to go.)

JILL: <u>I'm feeling kind of bad. Are you mad about something?</u> (Jill's counselor told her to tell him how she feels, and to ask him if she isn't sure how he feels, which is what she does.)

JACK: <u>You're the one who can't take "yes, we'll go," for an answer.</u> (Jack **judges**, **blocks**, and again **diverts** [doesn't answer the question]). He **accuses** Jill of not accepting his answer and **blames** her, suggesting she won't accept his agreement to go. Nothing makes a real woman more real—thus, displacing the dream woman—than her own expression of feelings. Jack feels attacked when the real woman shows up where his dream woman is supposed to be and he can't find her—that is, the rest of himself.)

JILL: <u>Never mind. I'll pick up some stuff at the market. They have some low-fat cheeses, and I think turkey would be good.</u> (She stops trying to explain, to understand, and to express her feelings. Starting fresh, Jill offers to shop for the picnic and tells Jack that she thinks certain foods would be good.)

JACK *(angrily)*: <u>That's not a picnic. We're not taking any diet stuff.</u> (Jack **defines** Jill's reality, assaulting her perceptions—to Jill, it *is* a picnic. And, with a unilateral decision, he **orders** her not to take the food she wants to take. Although Jack agreed to go on the picnic, he did it as if he were forced to agree. Then, to agree to what Jill wanted to take would have been recognizing the real woman as separate for the third time—thus, three times disconnecting himself from his dream woman.)

JILL: <u>I'll pick up whatever you want. I'll eat the low-fat stuff.</u> (Jill offers to get Jack whatever he wants, along with what she wants. She knows that if she can't even take her own food, something is seriously wrong. It seems so unreasonable. She tries to maintain her own reality by saying she'll eat her choice and that Jack will have his choice. She doesn't know about his dream woman, so she can't understand why he isn't happy that she'll shop for him.)

JACK: <u>And we'll end up with two picnic baskets, and I'm not lugging all that stuff out from the car. Just get some fried chicken, potato salad, and stuff.</u> (Jack **defines** the future and refuses to be part of it, **ordering,** not asking, Jill to get just what he wants. He cannot accept the real woman a fourth time. Still, he claims that it is because of the picnic baskets that he orders Jill to get only what he wants.)

JILL: <u>Okay, I'll keep the low-fat stuff separate in the little cooler and I'll carry it.</u> (Jill again agrees, saying, "okay," and handles Jack's dire prediction by telling him that she'll carry her choice of food. She thinks that will solve the problem. She thinks that he *really is* concerned about carrying two baskets. She doesn't know that his concern is not about carrying the baskets; it's about his having to recognize the real woman four times: once to agree to go on the picnic, once to accept that Jill's taste in food is not the same as his/dream woman's; and finally to carry the baskets.)

JACK: <u>Yeah, I bet you will. I'll end up carrying everything.</u> (Jack expresses doubt about Jill's honesty, and reaffirms his original scenario. This way he **counters** Jill who, in his mind, is wrong, simply because she won't be his dream woman. In order to make her wrong, he assumes that there will be more to carry because she wants diet food.)

JILL: <u>I don't see why you'd think that. I just told you I'd carry my stuff.</u> (Jill can't understand why he would think she was lying and reaffirms her offer.)

JACK: <u>Oh, sure! Like when we went to the fair.</u> (Jack again subtly **accuses** Jill of lying and brings up an occasion where he carried things. Now he can totally avoid his real feeling of losing his dream woman, and he can convince himself and Jill that his reluctance to let her buy diet food is all about his having to carry two baskets. It's really about her showing a sign of separateness by having different tastes from him, therefore, not being his dream woman.)

JILL: <u>But I had my niece in the stroller, and we had the luggage.</u> (Jill tries to explain how the two occasions are different.)

JACK: <u>Do you have to argue over everything? We can't even discuss a simple picnic without your complaints and arguments!!</u> (Jack **accuses** Jill of arguing, complaining, and not discussing the topic.)

JILL: <u>Look, I'll carry everything if you want. It's no problem. I'm not complaining.</u> (Jill tries to understand Jack, to address the topic, and says that if Jack thinks carrying the picnic basket is a problem, she doesn't see it as one. She also explains herself: that she isn't complaining.)

JACK *(sarcastically)*: <u>Huh, not complaining! Didn't you just tell me you were feeling sooo bad? And you had to bring your niece into it, just to argue.</u> (Jack **counters** Jill and accuses her of complaining and arguing. He speaks in an **abusively angry** way because he has not been able to erase the real woman and reconstitute the dream woman.)

JILL: <u>Jack, please listen. I'm going to get what you want. All I want is to have a nice day.</u> (Jill asks Jack to hear her, offers again, and tells him what she wants.)

JACK: <u>And you think I don't!</u> (Jack **accuses** Jill, again telling her what she thinks. He feels angry but doesn't know why so confabulates a reason for his anger: that she is thinking ill of him.)

JILL: <u>Jack, please, just tell me: Why do you think that I think you don't want to have a nice day? What have I said or done to give you that impression?</u> (Jill takes Jack's words for truth. She thinks he is rational and that he really thinks that she thinks that he doesn't want to have a nice day. Jill asks Jack two questions: why he thinks ill of her, and what gave him the impression that she felt he didn't want to have a nice day. She feels Jack's hostility and is confused. Not knowing about his dream woman, she doesn't know why she can't show Jack that she really is on his side and isn't the enemy.)

JACK: <u>I don't have to stand for this interrogation. Go on. Go to the store.</u> (Jack **accuses** Jill of ill will, an interrogation, and gives her **orders**.)

JILL: <u>I'm just trying to understand.</u> (Jill really is.)

JACK: <u>You always have to have the last word. You always have to have it your way. I'm really tired of this.</u> (Jack **accuses** Jill of arguing for the sake of arguing, of "wanting her way," and expresses his exasperation, **blaming** her for his anger and frustration.)

JILL: <u>But I'm not trying to have the last word.</u> (Jill tries again to explain her intentions.)

JACK: <u>There! Didn't you just do it again?</u> [*Very sarcastically:*] <u>"I'm not trying to have the last word."</u> (Jack **accuses** her again, and his sarcasm reveals **abusive anger.**)

JILL: <u>I'm going to the store. I feel so confused when I try to talk with you.</u> (Jill gives up trying to understand and trying to explain herself. She expresses her confusion.)

JACK: <u>Have it your way. Blame me. Boy, I'm really tired of your attacks.</u> (Jack again implies that Jill is selfish. He **criticizes** her, **accusing** Jill of being the one who is blaming, and he **accuses** her of attacking him.)

JILL: <u>What do you mean? What do you mean?</u> (Jill still hopes to understand.)

JACK: <u>If you don't know, then there's no use in my explaining. This conversation is over.</u> (Jack **withholds.** He **blames** Jill for not understanding and **blocks** all communication with a unilateral decision.)

Jack walks out.

This scenario illustrates the importance of the partner repeating a question that her mate either refuses to answer or answers with a question. If Jill knew about the dream woman, she would have asked, "Honey, I was wondering: Do you have any plans for tomorrow?" until he answered her question.

Of course, he could refuse to respond. If he doesn't respond, he is not relating to Jill. Jack and Jill don't have a relationship. They may or not may have a relationship in the future.

If her first question had been, "Do you want to go on a picnic tomorrow?" Jack likely would not have answered it any differently than he did her question about plans. His typical response would have been to ask a question. For instance, "Why are you asking me at the last minute? You know I've planned to do stuff around here on Saturday." Or, "Why would I want to go on a picnic?"

By repeating the question, Jill would not be diverted. She would not have to explain that she didn't know what he'd "planned to do . . ." She would not have to respond to pretend talk. No one on Earth knows what she knows. When Jack, in this version of the picnic scenario, says, "You know I've planned . . ." he is stepping into her very mind and telling her what she knows. This is what people do when they live within another person. This is what they do when they are so bereft of themselves they have "no leg to stand on," as the saying goes. This is why they may be thought of as psychological paraplegics. This is what they do when they have a dream woman who knows what they know, who has been with them since they were young (more about this in the next chapter).

If Jill had simply said, incredulously, "What?" or "What did you say?" when she heard statements like, "You've always got to have the last word," or "You've always got to have it your way," Jack might hear what he said and change it. If not, and if he repeats it, "You heard me. You've always got to have the last word," she might try a bit more. For instance, "What? Honey, you aren't me, so you don't know what I've got to have." If Jack insists on defining her inner reality, for instance, when he said, "And you think I don't!" Jill's response might be, "What? Honey, you aren't me, so you don't know what I think." As a last resort, she might say, "Honey, it is really scary to me to see you pretending to be me, telling me what I think, want, know, and so forth. You are not a woman. So please don't pretend to be one."

Let us now look at what I call "the switch"—the process by which the abuser anchors his dream woman in his partner's body/mind/soul. Once he has done that, he must silence his partner so he can go on with his dream woman.

THE SWITCH

Almost always, there is a time in an abusive relationship when it isn't abusive. Then one day, the man who becomes verbally abusive switches from being charming and kind to being verbally abusive and controlling. The trigger may be that his partner says she loves him, or they become engaged, or they marry, or the partner stays home to have a child. Now, his unconscious, if it could speak, says, "This body won't leave me now. It's a safe harbor for my dream woman."

There are many events that could trigger the switch. Here is an example that baffled one partner. After five years of marriage, her husband took out a very large insurance policy on himself, because, he said, "he was older and she should have some security." But their relationship changed drastically in a few weeks' time. He switched from being nice and respectful to angry and abusive. From our perspective, he must have felt very secure, secure enough to anchor his dream woman in his wife. If his unconscious could speak, it might have said, "This body won't leave me now. Who would walk away from a million dollars?" And, of course, once his dream woman was anchored in his partner, he could no longer see or hear the real woman (his partner). She only got in the way, and so of course he became angry and abusive.

Many relationships deteriorate and break up because of the rapid change that takes place in the relationship when a man suddenly experiences the security and even, sometimes, the euphoria of knowing he has secured his partner—a body for his dream woman. Some women can pinpoint the day that the switch took place.

Flora is one such woman. She said she had just gotten out of the hospital, where she had stayed overnight after her fiancé beat her up. She said that they had dated for several years, traveled the world, lived a life of privilege, and then suddenly he flew into a rage. "Why? What happened?" she asked. "I've already called off the engagement."

I asked, "What happened yesterday, before he hit you?"

She said, "We were at a small party and my bridesmaid was showing me a special makeup trick for the wedding. I said, 'Just a sec,' when he said something to me, and then he totally went nuts—sent everyone home, threw me across the room."

"But besides that," I said. "Something happened earlier that made him feel more secure. Can you think of what happened?"

"Well," Flora said, "we sent out three hundred wedding invitations to our friends and relatives all over the world."

"That's it!" I said. "If his unconscious could speak, it would have said, "With all the people invited, this one won't leave me now; she is a safe harbor for my dream woman." Then his dream woman poured into you, and he could no longer see *you*, the real person, any longer. From his perspective, at an unconscious level, you became the rest of himself—his unlived self. He no longer saw you through the vision of his dream woman. You now were his dream woman. Later, when he didn't have your instant, undivided attention, he lost that part of himself that he had anchored in you—his dream woman, who would always give him instant attention. He felt like he'd been attacked. He was enraged. All the time before when you were dating and engaged, he saw you through the lens of his dream woman—through the perfect vision. So, of course, he admired you and would do anything to win you. He courted you, until he felt he had you. Then unconsciously you *were* his dream woman and he could not see or hear you, the real woman, anymore."

In summary, drastic change in the abuser's behavior is the result of his anchoring his dream woman in his partner. He no longer sees the real woman through the vision of his dream woman, more wonderful than anyone else; basically, essentially, to him she *is* his dream woman, that is, his unlived self. And from that moment on, he cannot fully see or hear the real woman again. The real partner no longer exists in his mind or his reality. When real woman shows up, his *world* falls apart, and he feels attacked.

A Drastic Switch

The following story illustrates the switch in an even more dramatic way. The woman, whom I'll call Colleen, saw her husband change from a charming friend to a raging maniac. The switch was instantaneous and dramatic. She was absolutely terrified and paralyzed when it happened. "It was like instant insanity," Colleen said. "It was so unexpected I couldn't grasp it. I was split between what I thought and what I felt, like I was in two different places at the same time."

She had known her husband throughout childhood and into high school. They were very best friends. While not lovers, they had a great connection. They talked nearly every day. She knew him well. After they went off to college, they lost contact. Then, ten years later they reconnected. She said, "I had prayed for and wanted the richness of a relationship in my life.

"We met and spent quality time together. I was very happy. Everything was great between us, and I believed God had answered my prayers. After seeing each other for about a year, we married.

"My new marriage completely shattered me. I encountered severe verbal abuse. Right after our wedding, he began to be very angry, accusatory, and blaming for no reason I could think of. I thought I had done something unconsciously to upset him." The man she married was gracious, charming, gentle, even-keeled, well-mannered, stable, and respectful of women. The man she woke up with the next morning was an extremely hostile, demanding, raging maniac.

She said, "It was like someone else had stepped into his body. When others were around he acted very normal. But the minute they were out of earshot, he would lean down, lower his voice, turn his face so they couldn't see, and seethe at me, 'Goddam it, you fucking bitch. I saw what you were doing.'"

"What?" she would ask.

"You know," he would say.

She didn't know.

No one saw. No one knew.

"*What is wrong with me?*" she thought. He wasn't mad at anyone else.

"By our honeymoon," Colleen said, "I was traumatized, in posttraumatic shock, suicidal, and did not know what was real and unreal. He traumatized, isolated, withheld, and terrorized, with episodes of nonstop verbal assault interspersed with kindness and tender moments. These glimpses gave me hope for change and also relief from pain and isolation. Then it would begin again.

"In those tender moments, I, who had just been abused, became grateful to him, like he was the hero for the moment, and gratitude flooded me. Then the assault would begin again. Although he became physically abusive, I could not name it that. He shoved me, pinned me to walls, tore clothing off me to scare and degrade me. And, he would speed when driving and laugh at my fear.

"As determined and strong as I had been, in less than four months, I had dwindled to a helpless, terrorized, traumatized person who believed all she had been told through the brain-washing effect of the verbal abuse. In the years before I had married him, I had survived many obstacles and challenges. It all felt 'erased,' and I was helpless. I did not feel I could hold any job, or even get one. It was all compounded by my belief in God, turning the other cheek, walking in love, returning good for evil."

Colleen told me that if sometime during the day, she went near him to touch his arm to find out what was wrong, he would recoil instantly with rage, and push her away. "Goddamn it! Get away," he'd say. It was as if she had stabbed him. But it was she who felt stabbed—in the heart.

If she said, "Are you okay?" "Did I do something?" "What's wrong?" He would yell, "Goddamn it, all you want to do is fight. Look at you. All you want to do is fight, you goddamn fucking bitch."

If she brought him coffee, he raged, "You knew I wanted you to leave it upstairs. Fuck you." If, the next morning, she brought it upstairs, he raged in her face, "You were supposed to put it in the office. Why are you so perverse?"

"I don't think anyone on the outside could really understand, unless they had the same thing happen to them. One would think I could have stood up to it, since I am so strong. It would seem that I should have seen him and what he was doing for what it was.

"Why was I so confused? Because I knew him so well, and he had never lied to me. And don't some people have a completely skewed perception of themselves? Don't some people stand up to sing in a contest on television, and show that they have no sense of music or even sound? They do not see themselves. Perhaps what he said was true. Perhaps I did not see myself.

"There just are not words to express my experience of verbal abuse and his Jekyll/Hyde behavior. I questioned myself and thought I was probably insane. I thought that every perception of who I thought I was must be wrong, and I was a sick, mean, controlling person—the most unlovable on the face of the earth. I hated me."

Later, Colleen said, "It was a 'soul rape.' If he could have taken out a piece of my soul and put a piece of his soul in mine, he would have. Much later, after the relationship ended, I came to see that he was out to destroy me so his dream person could enter my soul/mind/emotions. And I would be programmed to do or be anything and everything he wanted at any moment. I had loved him so much. I would have done anything reasonable, if he had asked. But now of course, I know he could not ask me because he could not see me.

"I had moments when I came out from under the 'trance' of his brainwashing, but it was glimmers. I also had glimmers when the relationship ended just months later. But I was almost nonfunctional by that point.

"Formerly successful, I now had almost no money, no job, no home, no understanding. I wanted to die. I had nonstop flashbacks, and it was as if he was still here, still abusing. It was like I was in and out of reality.

"Now, years later, it still seems incomprehensible that someone could be like that. It is so heinous."

Colleen had experienced extreme trauma, and because of the tender and kind moments, she also trauma-bonded to him. Much like Stockholm syndrome, it imprisons the mind and consciousness, the soul and spirit of the victim.

A similar story arrived in the mail today. The writer, who divorced after her children were grown, said, "The biggest mistake of my whole life was not to have left my ex-husband within the first four hours of the wedding ceremony."

The verbally abusive man avoids his partner's existence by giving her the silent treatment or by defining her in some way. Just as the man from the 1850s who defined his wife as "not capable" of voting, the abuser may try to undermine his partner so that he can silence her and stop her independent actions—actions that do not match his dream woman's actions. Or he may deny and counter her perceptions and opinions by telling her that they are wrong. If she objects, he will tell her that something is wrong with her or what she is trying to do. If she defends herself by explaining herself to him or by telling him how she feels, he may become overtly threatening and in doing so, gradually destroy her self-perception even as he silences her.

Knowing about the dream woman relieves the partner of any lingering doubts that she has said or done something to worsen her relationship, or has failed to do or say something that would have improved it. Knowing that the verbally abusive man defines his partner to silence her so that he can be with his dream woman can relieve much of her confusion. Otherwise, she is stuck with the old clichés: He's insecure. He secretly feels inferior to women so he is dominating. He thinks he is much more important than any woman, and entitled. While in some cases these clichés may contain some truth, they do not explain his behavior.

3

TYPES AND ORIGINS OF VERBAL ABUSE

THERE ARE TWO ENDS OF a spectrum of abusive behavior: covert (hidden) and overt (obvious). Some men who indulge in verbal abuse are clearly at the covert end of the spectrum, while others are at the overt end. Some indulge in both types of abusive behaviors, spanning the entire spectrum.

There are some general differences between men who indulge in covert verbal abuse versus overt. The abuser's behavior—whether he employs overt or covert means—is determined by how old he was when he began forming his dream woman. The critical factor is his age when he was most damaged—that is, when he lost touch with himself and began to bury his experiences and all attributes ascribed to the feminine. Let's see how this works.

THE COVERT VERBAL ABUSER

If he was very young when he was most damaged, then he started forming a dream woman and building a buried self at that tender age. The dream woman, as I've described, is simply the personification of his unlived, unintegrated self. She is personified just like a young child would perceive the feminine to be: an all-needs-meeting mother.

Clients often say something like, "I can handle the money, come and go when I want, but my husband is irritated or angry with me most of the time, and I feel like I'm losing my mind."

I'll ask, "Does he counter or object to all your thoughts, opinions, and ideas?"

"Constantly," they will reply.

Then I'll ask, "Does he put you down, but say it is just a joke, or that you don't have a sense of humor?"

They invariably say, "Yes, it's so hard to pin it down. He says I can't take a joke. On the other hand, even when he's angry at who knows what, he doesn't hit me, or physically threaten me, but I feel like I'm walking on eggshells."

"I can understand that you would, not knowing what will set him off," I say to them. "Tell me this: Does he help bring in the groceries, and even help you load the dishwasher or clear the table, or things like that?"

"Oh yes, he tries to be helpful, but he gets irritated and snaps at me all the time."

"Well," I'll say, "I would guess that he doesn't tell you what to wear and where you can go. Is that right?" I ask.

"Yes," invariably it is.

As a general rule, this type of covert abuser started forming his dream woman when he was very little, and as such, this dream woman is personified as an all-needs-meeting mother. Consequently, he treats his partner like a child treats his mother.

Mother can handle the money, work, go to meetings, and so forth. So, the partner does these things without his objection. He doesn't hit her or call her vile names because the child rarely hits his mother or calls her names. Instead, he ignores the real woman so that he can stay in the dream state with his dream woman, who has the qualities of a mother who meets his every need.

Even though he is not controlling about her activities, there is a great problem in the relationship. Since he and his dream woman have been together in his psyche since he was a baby, he is extremely dependent on keeping her alive and well in his partner. He is caught up in keeping his partner from getting angry and leaving, so he will be helpful in many situations, but he cannot allow her to be a separate person. Since he started forming his dream woman when he was very young, she is a big part of him. Consequently, a real woman's separateness is a great threat to him. How dare she have different thoughts and opinions? He must pretend not to hear them or to negate and erase them from his partner's mind. Hence, he ignores her entirely or argues against everything she says.

Furthermore, since he and his dream woman are of the same mind—his—if she has a really good idea, it has to be his, because there is no way he will accept her separateness. Her ideas, or solutions to problems, or funny jokes, are all his. She gets no credit for them. He seems not to hear her, and then later comes up with them as if they were his ideas or jokes.

He must erase the real woman's thoughts, counter and discount her experiences, because they don't match his. If he cannot silence her, his rage may be so great that he will not speak to her for days, even weeks, in some cases, never addressing the real woman at all. By pretending she doesn't exist, he copes with her realness and manages his anger, always walking away when she is talking, always refusing to answer her questions about him. In this way, he preserves his primal connection to his dream woman, who already knows everything about him. One common way of not answering is by diverting any question with another question. He simply asks a question to sidetrack the conversation. He must do this because if he responded to the real woman he would be acknowledging her, severing himself from the rest of himself, committing emotional suicide.

It is important for the partner to really understand and know that this mate has a psychological disability. He is so disconnected through trauma, training, and trying to not feel, that at the extreme he is like a psychological paraplegic.

Enduring the silent treatment—a state of nonrelationship—with a spouse or life partner is confusing and painful. The covertly abusive man is caught between keeping his partner happy, "I let you do what you want, don't I?" and pretending she doesn't exist as a separate person. A separate thought by the real woman would sever him from his dream woman, and he wouldn't be able to find her.

Telling the real woman that she doesn't know what she is talking about, or that she is imagining things, or that she doesn't have a sense of humor are his predominate ways of denying the abuse. He rarely if ever indulges in physical abuse or gives his partner orders the way overt abusers usually do. He might, however, if he is at the extreme, be capable of violence. If his partner suddenly seems to be leaving or taking attention away from him, he could feel like he was being killed—and kill back. In that case, if he had no other body around for his dream woman, no lover in the wings, he might kill himself because he lost the rest of himself when he killed his dream woman.

THE OVERT VERBAL ABUSER

On the other end of the spectrum, the overt verbal abuser may call his partner names and may escalate to physical abuse. The overt verbal abuser doesn't mind giving orders because it's not "Mom" he's talking to. It is more like Barbie. He shows more anger and keeps her from getting away through threats and intimidation. He rages at his partner, calls her names, restricts her movements, controls her money, and tracks her actions because he formed his dream woman near puberty, and she is not an all-needs-meeting mother. His dream woman, the personification of his unlived self, is a teen's perception of the feminine: a femme fatale, a beauty queen, and a dream woman in every sense— a "young thing" he can direct and control who has no life outside of his own. She is a doll, a beautiful object he can gloat over and possibly throw around or beat up if he can't find other ways to control her, or if she seems to act like a separate and real person.

Usually, the overt verbal abuser feels that he is superior to women and has the right to be in charge of his partner. He may denigrate women because he secretly doubts his masculinity and so defines himself as "not like a woman." He may have felt unacceptable to his father or the male world if he didn't have a warm accepting father, or if he was rejected in some way, or if he lost his father in his preteen or teen years. In some cases, while he demeans the feminine, he fears that he might be seen as "like a woman." This would be most likely if he was sexually assaulted as a teenager.

Some verbally abusive men move between the two poles of covert and overt verbal abuse. They more or less combine them, countering their partner's every thought, and also threatening and intimidating her if she objects.

The model of the dream woman, the abuser's unlived self, and his bond to her, help to explain his abusive and controlling behaviors. Of course, he is unaware of how horrifying his behavior is to his partner. When he can't find his dream woman, or when there is even the threat of not finding her, he feels horribly attacked. He may explode in rage or, alternatively, if he is covert, hide his anger, even from himself, by refusing to acknowledge that a real woman even exists.

The two extremes of verbal abuse, overt and covert, portray how the verbally abusive man may behave unpredictably, irrationally, frighteningly, strangely, and hurtfully while completely unprovoked by his partner. In fact, it is her rational, real, honest, down-to-earth authenticity that most often triggers his abuse. After all, the more real she is, the more she takes up space and shows up in the body where he anchored his dream woman. And the dire consequence (to him) is that he then can't find the rest of himself.

THE INSIDE AND OUTSIDE WORLDS

Intimate or domestic violence is often a surprise to those outside the relationship who believed that they really knew the perpetrator. But the abuser acts very differently around people who are not part of his dream world. His family, wife, and children are a dream family. He has a dream partner and likely has dream children, although not always. Those on the outside of his dream world are in the rest of the world, the real one.

The verbal abuser perfected his image or persona and developed his identity according to what the world that he knew expected of him. The outside world—that is, the rest of the world—must always affirm his persona. It is as if he has a world of close people (dream people) on the inside and a world of others (real people) on the outside.

The verbally abusive man flips back and forth between the inside world, composed of family or other close people, and the outside world, the real one. He can become terrified, filled with rage, or violent if even the possibility exists that the outside world might see what goes on in his inside world. He is not usually aware of this dichotomy, but to exist in the outside world, he must have the identity he developed there. His identity or image might be one of affability, kindness, magnanimity, and strength. As a result, he may switch back and forth between verbal abuser and his nice guy persona. For instance, he may be angry with his partner and then suddenly very nice to a neighbor who comes to the door to borrow something.

The abuser's two worlds do not meet. Yet the partner knows nothing of his two worlds. Most commonly, she seeks mutuality, that is, a win-win solution to problems. In most cultures, as she was growing up, she was allowed her inner world. She could have feelings and express them. She could have intuition; in fact, some cultures believe that intuition is "a girl thing." She was allowed her sensate awareness. She didn't have to be tough. Consequently, she does not have a huge unlived self—unless she has been severely traumatized. Because she was allowed to develop as a normal human being and was trained to "think of the other person first," to "give more than you get," to "give the other person the benefit of the doubt," or "love heals all," she tries to make sense of her adult relationship and to make it work. But the verbally abusive man is often coldly distant or angry because she just never quite matches his dream woman, and when he can't find his dream woman he feels irritated or attacked. His attempts to keep his dream woman viable within his partner are extremely controlling. Often, even the partner has difficulty recognizing the abuse. He and his partner are living in two different realities. His is one of power over her. Hers is one of mutuality. These are the two realities, Reality One and Reality Two, which I described in my first book, *The Verbally Abusive Relationship*.

Not only does the partner find it difficult to understand her relationship because her mate is in a different reality, she also finds it difficult to explain her experience to the outside world because outsiders don't see it. Many women have said, in effect, "No one else knew how things really were. It was like my husband was two different people: one, when he was with me, and a different, completely happy-go-lucky, charming person for almost everyone else." And sometimes not even the children see it.

"Everything appears normal with everyone else and in every other situation," said one woman. "He seems normal, rational, and sane with everyone but me, and it is most terrifying."

Ultimately, verbal abuse destroys minds and brainwashes people until they become convinced that they are at fault, and are intrinsically flawed and unworthy.

HOW DID HE GET THE WAY HE IS?

It is a popular theory that men who abuse their partners were not necessarily abused in childhood, but I have heard from hundreds of verbally abusive men, and I have never found one who had a kind, nondefining, accepting father. Men who become verbally abusive often were verbally abused themselves so that they became disconnected from their feelings, sensations, and intuitions. Some defining statements follow.

> "You're being a wuss."
> "Quit being a wimp."
> "You're being a fag."
> "Don't be such a girl."
> "You're not hurt."
> "Now you're being a sissy."
> "You have nothing to cry about."
> "You'll never amount to anything."
> "You're trying to get out of it."
> "You're being a baby."
> "You're just trying to get attention."
> "You're not listening."

"Suck it up."

"Get over it."

"You like to whine."

Alternatively, his father stood by when his mother verbally abused him and did nothing but gain some vicarious control of his son through his wife. Other examples of abuse are:

- He was ridiculed when he expressed himself and so came to believe that his perceptions and feelings were insignificant.
- His father mocked him or called him names when he expressed pain and sadness.
- His father ignored him and thereby gave him the message that he was nonexistent, unacceptable, or worthless.
- His father demeaned qualities ascribed to the feminine, such as nurturance, receptivity, and empathetic expressions, so he did too.
- He heard his father try to control his mother through anger and verbal abuse and thereby determined that having power over the feminine kept one safe from similar ridicule.
- His father was absent or not accepting of him in his first ten years.
- His father physically assaulted him, his father did nothing to stop his mother from physically assaulting him, or both parents physically assaulted him.

In nearly all cases, the abuser's father or father figure did not accept his emotions when he was little. His father told him that he should not feel the way he felt, especially when he cried or was upset. If he was afraid of something or someone, instead of getting comfort and support, he was put down for his natural feelings. If he went to his father for comfort and affection—a hug, for instance—he was pushed away.

His father often criticized him when he didn't perform like his dream son. For instance, he told him that what he did was not the way he should have done it. It could be anything: the way he cleaned his room, mowed the lawn, or performed in sports. Typically, while his father's criticism was constant, praise was rare. In order to shape him into his dream son, his father also called him names and thereby told him that he was not who he was, but was something entirely different. In all or any of these ways his father defined him, leaving him with an "unlived self."

IS THERE A GENETIC COMPONENT?

The pattern—not seeing one's partner, looking for the dream woman, raging when she's lost, or ignoring the real woman completely—can be passed down from one generation to another by men who deny the emotional, intuitive, and even sensate lives of their sons. I want to emphasize that abuse, unless it originates with some rare genetic mishap, is not passed on with genes. It is passed on by abusive behavior.

The verbally abusive man was influenced to lose himself, or disconnect from his experiences and emotions, either because of the absence of his father, or because he was verbally abused by his father. For example, every father who tells his son that he is "a crybaby," "a wuss," "being a fag" or "a girl for crying" is not only verbally abusing his son, he is disconnecting him from his true self and his inner world, from his feeling, sensate, and intuitive functions. This father is rejecting his real son and is angry that he is losing his dream son, the part of himself that he lost when his own father abused him. He cannot see his son as a real person, and so in defining his son, he ends his relationship with him. At the same time, he is creating a puppet son, who is empty inside, performing as he directs.

A man took the time to write to me and graciously gave me permission to quote him. He knew that just as his grandfather had rejected his father, creating the unlived self that became the dream woman whom his father sought, not only in his wife, but also in other women, he had done the same. Here is how he described his knowledge of generations of abuse and his recognition that *his changing is essential.*

"I'm a man who as a child, was subjected to verbal and physical abuse from my father. He also verbally and physically abused my mother and my other siblings. My mom, being of the old-school train of thought, worshipped the ground this man walked on. I recall her on her deathbed, begging him to tell her he loved her. She was his slave; all the while, he beat her, cheated on her, and berated and belittled us all. My grandfather on my father's side was the same way. Now my son is very abusive, and I must change myself and help him to change as well."

Men who have been abusive and are aware of it want to do what they can to help other men see the evil root that grows an abuser; that evil root is, of course, verbal abuse itself. Unfortunately, verbal abuse doesn't usually look horrible to those standing on the sideline. Only the person targeted realizes its destructive force. And often for the partner, the pain is too real and too late to avoid. Hence, the old nursery rhyme about Peter, a covert means of teaching a boy to isolate his partner, and teaching the girl to be kept and isolated.

> Peter, Peter, pumpkin eater,
> Had a wife and couldn't keep her;
> He put her in a pumpkin shell,
> And there he kept her very well.

The ways that men define women, the stress such psychic intrusions create, the destruction of familial relationships, the addictive escapes from such abuse, the emotional pain and mental anguish tell us that *his changing is essential.* Even so, most men who are motivated to change are motivated by a different perspective. Their primary motivation is that they do not want to lose the body that harbors their dream woman. This motive may lead to more genuine motives later on if the verbally abusive man begins the work that change requires. Unless he can do the work, however, he will simply strive to keep the body for his dream woman.

Men who are most disconnected from their inner world and who most need to live within their partners, defining them as if they *were* their partners, often desperately seek to feel superior to women by making up a story that God has put them in charge of their partners. Silly story that it is, it is also a dangerous and desperate act of undeveloped, unintegrated men. Adults may be in charge of children but not other adults.

The verbally abusive man may have a kind and loving mother or an abusive mother who increased his disconnection from himself. No matter how good a mother he has or had, the primary and sometimes the only influence on the son is his father. In other words, a mother cannot really reverse damage done by the father, no matter how she tries, and no matter how much she tells her son, "Daddy really loves you, he just doesn't know how to show it, and he didn't mean what he said." If, however, she stands up for her children in front of her spouse, saying something like, "Hey, what did you say? This is a safe house. There'll be no putdowns here," she may prevent much damage and be a strong influence on her children.

NOW WE KNOW—OF COURSE

Once the dream woman is anchored in his partner, verbal abuse is the automatic and expected outcome of a man's attempts to keep his unlived self—that is, his dream woman—alive. He will tell the real woman how she should be. He will confabulate reasons for the horrible feeling he has when he can't find his dream woman, telling the real woman that she has done something to him. He will pretend that the real woman doesn't exist by refusing to speak to her. All of this is controlling behavior.

Without a doubt, if we look at a verbally abusive relationship through the dream woman paradigm, we see exactly what is going on in the everyday life of the verbally abusive man and his partner. Here are some of the behaviors that confuse and wound the partner of a verbally abusive man and the reasons for them.

"He often walks away in the middle of a conversation, like we weren't talking and like I suddenly don't exist."

Of course he will walk away when you are talking to him. Then he can stay in the dream state with his dream woman and not risk losing the rest of himself.

"He doesn't do what he promises to do."

Of course he will say, "Yeah, yeah, yeah, I'll do it," then not do it. By saying, yes, he'll do it, he shuts up the real woman and can stay in the dream state with his dream woman. By *not* doing it, he can avoid *acting* as if the real woman is real.

"He is nice to everyone else, but not to me."

Of course he acts unkindly to you and kindly to others; he hasn't anchored a dream person in neighbors or colleagues.

"Instead of being empathetic, he gets mad when I tell him what bothers me."

Of course he is angriest when you are most real, most heartfelt, trying most to get his understanding; then you really show up and are, therefore, most displacing of his dream woman. And the real woman's thoughts are irrelevant since she "should" think what he thinks.

"He acts differently in front of others."

Of course he acts differently in front of others. He built his persona of looking good from the outside in, so he has to look good in the outside world.

"He claims I say and do things that I haven't said or done."

Of course he claims you've said and done things that you haven't; he has to confabulate reasons for his anger since he doesn't know about his dream woman.

"He will not answer a direct question about himself."

Of course he won't answer a direct question about himself because his dream woman already "knows" him.

"Sometimes, quite unpredictably, he cuts me to the quick with a cruel comment."

Of course he will put you down for no reason at all; by putting *you* down, there is more room in your body for his dream woman.

"He doesn't ask with a 'please.' When he wants something, I almost have to guess what that is."

Of course he will not ask directly with a please for something he would like; his dream woman already knows what he wants because they've been together since he was young.

"He argues against everything I say, all my opinions, views, and preferences."

Of course he counters your very thoughts; his dream woman and he are of the same mind—his.

"He won't let me have my own opinion."

Of course he gets very angry when you have a different opinion because he can't find his dream woman, who thinks what he thinks; furthermore, he has lost the "rest of himself" that he anchored in you.

"He doesn't ask me about me. It's as if he has no interest in me."

Of course he seldom, if ever, asks you about you: how you feel, what you like about a restaurant, what you thought about a movie, or what your favorite flower is. Doing so would conjure up a real woman in the body where he anchored his dream woman. She'd be displaced. He would feel like he had lost part of himself.

"He gets really, really angry, even rages, for no clear reason."

Of course he gets hysterical when he can't find his dream woman; she is the rest of him and he can't live without her.

"I can't remember him ever apologizing for his behavior."

Of course he won't apologize for his behavior; to him it is nothing compared to your "audacity" to appear as a real woman. To him, your appearance as a real woman where his dream woman is supposed to be is an attack on him.

"When I don't have the same opinion that he has, like about political issues, and I don't change it to his opinion, he tells me I'm stubborn. Why would he care if I have a different opinion?"

Of course he wants you to have the same opinion he has. He and his dream woman have been together virtually all his life, and she always thinks what he thinks and believes what he believes. Your having a different opinion feels like an attack, and he is convinced that you should change your mind and that you are just trying to be hurtful and difficult and therefore, stubborn, if you don't change it. It is your mind, of course, that he tries to control, including your thinking and your decision-making processes.

"He tells me that I know what he meant when I really don't know what he meant."

Of course he thinks you know what he meant. He holds as reality the idea that you are of one mind with him, or, conversely, that he is you.

"When I try to explain that I didn't do or say something that he's angry about, he always says I'm wrong in some way."

Of course he says you're wrong; he knows what his dream woman should do and he sees you as making an excuse, being the plaintiff coming to him with your plea, as the plea of a plaintiff in a court of law. In other words, hearing your explanation, he sees himself as both the judge and jury who listen to your pleas. Unfortunately, since, in this scenario, he is both the judge and jury, he will rule in his own favor every time.

"He is always worse when he's drinking."

Of course verbal abusers are more abusive under the influence of alcohol; they are less connected inside, more "beside themselves," and therefore, they have more of themselves (dream woman) anchored in their partners and become more enraged when the real woman shows up. Just as the abuser anchors his dream woman in his partner when he feels that she won't leave him, he may also withdraw his dream woman when she seems to be an unsafe harbor for this part of himself. When he is beside himself, he totally depends on his dream woman being his partner. He literally and figuratively can't stand on his own two feet.

"After a crisis point, he tells me he'll love me forever and that he wants me back."

Of course he feels that he loves you and wants you back. He sees you through the vision of his dream woman, and you look better than ever before. But once you are back and he feels secure, he will reanchor his dream woman in you more deeply than ever before because he will feel that by coming back, you have *chosen* him. He is more secure.

In summary, when his partner has left or is about to leave, the verbally abusive man unconsciously withdraws his dream woman from her, and he begins to see her through the beautiful vision of his dream woman. His dream woman is no longer *in* his partner, but is right there in front of him. Seeing his partner through the vision of his dream woman is like looking through rose-colored glasses. She's looking better than ever before. She is infinitely desirable; she is everything he ever wanted—the rest of himself, so to speak. He will say and do anything to get back the body that harbored his dream woman—unless, that is, he has already found a new body for her. If this is the case, he may even find one that looks the same as his partner. For instance, if she was slim, blue-eyed with long blond hair, he will look for the same body in the next women he goes after.

WHY HE DOES IT, FROM HIS POINT OF VIEW

Aside from the ways he defines his partner, he may tell her why he does what he does. This may occur on occasions when he has left a record of his abuse, for instance, on voice mail, or because his partner had an audiotape on. Since he cannot deny the abuse, he explains it. Here are some examples from real verbal abusers:

- "I keep hurting you 'cause you keep bouncing back."
- "I don't believe in all this feel-good stuff . . . spirit killing, healing tears stuff."
- "I don't care about your feelings . . . I could care less."
- "Nothing matters to me . . . I don't give a fuck what you want."

And of course he doesn't.

4

DOES COUNSELING HELP? SOME THERAPISTS DON'T KNOW

CERTAINLY, THERE ARE SOME SUPERB therapists, psychologists, psychiatrists, counselors, ministers, priests, and rabbis who understand verbally abusive relationships and who are helping people recover from painful experiences.

Everyday, however, I hear from women who have tried in vain to find a therapist who understands what verbally abusive relationships actually are. They want someone who can help them bring about some tangible change in their mates. They are looking for someone who can validate their experiences. These women want someone to help them recover, at least enough to have the strength to leave their mate if he can't change. And, if they've left their relationship, they want help in getting past the trauma they experienced. They need help starting a new life, to recover from posttraumatic stress and sometimes from trauma bonding.

The stress of a verbally abusive relationship is unbearable, and no woman expects it to happen to her. Almost every woman in such a relationship who contacts me is very well educated and either is in a career or has set it aside to raise her children. I am always surprised when someone tells me that they thought it didn't happen to people in higher socioeconomic circumstances. No matter how successful their marriage looks from the outside, or how lucky they are told they are to have such wonderful husbands, there are millions of women who feel like they are going crazy in their relationships and, of course, some men are too. I am certain that 95 percent of them saw no signs of abuse before their spouses switched on them.

Here is where therapy can be supportive and very helpful to the partner of a verbally abusive man. Healing begins when the partner is no longer subjected to verbal abuse. Either the verbal abuser stops abusing, or the partner has no contact with him. Good supportive therapy by a therapist who understands, and perhaps a trauma therapist, can help women recover from verbally abusive relationships.

When women are in relationships that they recognize as verbally abusive, they often think, "Maybe a therapist can help us get our relationship to work." One woman told me, "If only he realized how hurtful his behavior is. If only he realized that I am not the enemy. If only he would listen when I explain to him how certain things he says are just not true about me. If only he would understand that a simple response like, 'I hear you on that,' or a simple expression of interest in me, 'Whatcha thinking about?' would, compared to what I get from him, be so incredibly heartwarming, and would so endear him to me. It would be great. It seems like a pretty simple thing. But now the things he says don't bring me closer to him; instead, his verbal abuse pushes me away.

Maybe a therapist can help me get him to see what he is doing. He didn't used to be like this. Not when I met him."

Unfortunately, when couples in these circumstances see a counselor who hasn't learned about verbally abusive relationships, they might very well be walking into an unsafe place. The counselor might hear verbal abuse in her or his own office, and, by not stopping it or even pointing it out, give tacit approval of it.

SHARING THE BLAME

Not only is observing abuse and not stopping it a problem, but possibly worse than that is the fact that many counselors are highly trained to conscientiously blame the victim, ascribing the problem and its cause equally to both husband and wife. Women who get their spouses to go with them to a counselor for help in dealing with verbal abuse and putting an end to it are sometimes told by these counselors that it is a "fifty-fifty" thing.

One woman told me, "Having read about control and verbal abuse, my husband is serving the facts to them on a platter: he does it; he knows he does it; he takes full responsibility for it (for once); it's not *my* fault; he will do *anything* (medication, if necessary—this from a man who hates doctors) to fix himself because though he may have lost me, he wants to be a better person and doesn't want to perpetuate this through his children. And what do the counselors still say? 'It's clear that you two harm each other emotionally'!"

Have these counselors ever read any literature on verbal abuse? My guess is probably not.

Women are often asked what their part in it is, and, ultimately, if their therapist is not aware of verbal abuse, they are told that if they were loving, they would be loved. Paradoxically, friends, columnists, talk-show hosts, and the culture at large ask these very same women, "Why do you stay in an abusive marriage?" Obviously, if the partner of an abuser is half-responsible and doesn't "love enough," and the partner believes these bizarre judgments, the partner may stay just to figure out what her part in the problem is. (Even magazine covers tell women "how to make your relationship better.")

"IT'S ALL YOUR FAULT"

But even worse, some women are told that it's not a fifty-fifty thing—that it's actually her fault that she is suffering and being yelled at and put down. In fact, if it weren't for the way she is, she would not be having the experiences she describes. A woman went in tears to a counselor after trying to figure out what was wrong and coming to the conclusion that she was in a verbally abusive relationship. Her counselor said, "Your relationship is in trouble. Your relationship is the garden. You are the gardener, and you haven't been tending the garden." Though the experiences are of abuse, this may not be clear to the counselor who might have been trained to define her just as her spouse defines her. Such training, though well meaning, may erroneously be based on the theory that if there is a problem in a relationship, both people contribute to it. This makes the victim feel crazy. It defines her as the cause, at least in part, of her own abuse. She may spend years trying to figure out what she is doing wrong, not realizing that it is only her existence that threatens the abuser. The pain she experiences originates with his attempts to shape her into his dream woman—an amorphous, ever-changing, needs-meeting part of himself.

Some women I've spoken with have even heard, "You let it happen. You asked for it. You allowed it in some way. You opened your life to Satan." These are all ridiculous statements and are all verbally abusive in and of themselves. They are psychic rapes, so to speak. No one can enter a person's psyche and tell her what she did.

Sometimes, in order to show a client how silly such statements are, I ask her to imagine that she went to a hospital for the mentally insane and picked out an inmate who seemed really nice. Then, when that inmate started exhibiting crazy behavior and she went to a counselor, the counselor said, "It's partly your fault. Try harder. It's a fifty-fifty thing." Even if she spent her life trying, would that inmate change?

Here is another example of blaming the victim. This woman, whom I'll call Betty, happened to call just as I was writing this chapter, so I asked her if I could use her story. She had just left her first meeting with a counselor this very morning, where she was told that in some way she has made her spouse verbally abusive.

Betty said that she went to therapy by herself, so she could explain what she was experiencing without fear of what her husband would say. She hoped that with the therapist's support, she could bring her husband in for the next appointment and the therapist would help her to help him see what he was doing. She told me about her husband's behavior and I thought it was definitely verbally abusive: He gave her orders, criticized her constantly, and countered her every thought, getting very angry when she tried to get him to stop. It turned out that her session with the therapist was not destined to work at all.

The therapist told Betty that she was encouraging her spouse to be emotionally dependent on her, and that caused him to feel hostile toward her, which was why he was so angry and cruel.

"Are you sure that's what your therapist said?" I asked.

"Yes," she said. "I questioned her further just to be clear about what she said."

"Did you ask her *how* you are making him emotionally dependent on you? Especially considering he travels three days a week, and you're busy with young children *and* getting career training when they're in preschool?"

How could Betty be making her husband dependent? Frankly, I couldn't imagine. And, neither, it seems, could the therapist. Betty *had* asked her therapist how she made her husband emotionally dependent. Betty had even asked for some idea of what she could change. She was willing to change *whatever it was* that made it her fault that her husband was so often inexplicably, fiercely angry with her. Betty's therapist never answered the all-important question. She diverted into a new topic instead.

I can only assume that Betty's therapist really didn't know why Betty's husband was abusive. I can only assume that maybe she had heard some theory about "husband dependence" and tried to make the case fit the theory, all because she had never learned about verbally abusive relationships.

Needless to say, Betty felt confused and depressed by the unproductive session with her therapist. When she called me, she was searching for answers. Did she actually have some behavior that made her husband dependent on her? Was she the cause of her husband's abuse? Can someone actually *make* another person abuse her or him?

Betty was confused, as she had already spent time and energy trying not to "make" her husband dependent on her because she was planning to leave him. She had stopped leaving casseroles when she wouldn't be home for dinner. She had stopped signing holiday cards with his name too—let him sign his own. She had asked him to do his own laundry and refill his coffee when he was in the kitchen. She tried to live as if she were alone, which of course she was, from the standpoint of not having a real relationship. She just did not want to be the cause of the abuse, as the therapist said, and she did not want her spouse to take her for granted. She hoped he would change, but she did not count on it. She was in survival mode.

Another woman, whom I'll call Judy, was told by a therapist that she could make her relationship work if she were just more pleasing. She told me, "It was a truly awful encounter with an awful therapist. I have felt so overwhelmed with responsibility, thinking and being told that it was up to me to fix this, that somehow I could fix it. Too much of my life energies have been used to figure this out, change myself, my environment, my husband, anything to make this better. Because surely if this was somehow my fault, it was my responsibility to fix it. Surely, if there was nothing wrong with my husband, then this awful dynamic must be *my* fault. I alternately rebelled against and believed that. I was deathly afraid to go to another counselor and be told the same thing. I felt I couldn't bear it."

Eventually Judy's husband admitted he had a problem. She was finally believed, and he found a therapist. He went and revealed his anger and abuse problems and asked for help. Judy was invited to go with him to talk to the therapist, and she did. There she said that she hoped to recover from the trauma in her own therapy. What did this therapist then say to her? She said that Judy had pulled back from her husband, so the therapist didn't think Judy seemed committed to the marriage and actually asked how her husband was supposed to be motivated to change if she wasn't committed. "What?" she asked. "What does my commitment have to do with him seeking help to become a healthier, whole human being? He has to change for himself, not for me."

Another woman who kept notes on what she heard, just to "stay sane," said that no counselor ever asked her what she heard, what she had written, or acted like it might be important. This was even after the woman told the counselor she had documented what happened.

Yet another woman was told by a counselor that she was codependent. She asked me, "Why did no counselor think to look at the dynamics within the marriage for clues to my unhappiness? Why, every time I talked about my husband's hurtful behaviors, did I get the whole mess dropped squarely on my shoulders?"

This counselor had no idea that a man might counter a woman's every thought and define her inner reality in order to shape her into his dream woman. This counselor had no idea that a man might rage when his partner doesn't appear as his dream woman—the amorphous, ever-changing part of himself that he has anchored in her. Codependency has nothing to do with a verbally abusive man verbally abusing his partner. He has the problem.

SOMETIMES COUNSELORS JUST DON'T KNOW

I make these points about counseling not working because it is an enormous problem. Couples counseling doesn't work when verbal abuse is the issue. Couples counseling is based on the assumption that both parties see and hear each other, period.

Read, for example, this bit of advice a woman received from her counselor: "Just be loving and affectionate; tell him how it hurts your feelings when he *yells* at you for no reason." The woman then said to me, "I'd like to see that counselor be on the receiving end of a 6-foot, 230-pound, 330-pound-bench pressing male's temper tantrum and say, 'That hurts my feelings'!"

When the partner expresses her feelings, the partner is never more real, as I discussed in the last chapter. Telling him how she feels is the last thing to do when she is being abused.

It's no wonder, then, that my clients question why, if change is so important, counselors and therapists haven't brought about change? Why is the defining of women in particular such an enormous problem? Is it a blind spot in the psychological community?

The short answer is that many counselors and therapists don't know about verbal abuse. In fact, after training hundreds of therapists and counselors in America and Australia, I realized that this information is news to many. But it is not the fault of therapists. Some therapists have learned about verbally abusive relationships by reading and researching on their own. But that is the exception, not the norm. Unless the counselor understands what is going on, and knows what to do about it, therapy is often of no use. Individual therapy, however, can be very beneficial for the man who indulges in verbal abuse. This will be described in Chapter 12, "The Process of Change." Individual counseling, where the couple sees the therapist separately, may also be helpful.

Usually, the educational process that culminated in the licensing of most therapists failed to even mention verbally abusive relationships. We'll find out why in the following pages. We will see why the problem of verbal abuse has been ignored for so long and why verbal abuse can show up right in front of some therapists but not be recognized for what it is.

A HISTORICAL PERSPECTIVE

Just for clarity, let's take a step back from the problem of change and briefly look at the pure ignorance that perpetuates verbal abuse. Taking a historical perspective can be helpful in understanding the scope of verbal abuse. Sometimes I will talk about the history of men defining women to a client who is devastated that her husband has been defining her. Yes, it is devastating, painful, and traumatizing, but it is also part of a pattern that has been socially sanctioned for generations. While women have been most defined as "not people" by means of exclusionary practices in years past, in current relationships, they face more direct attempts to annihilate their consciousness.

What was going on when men developed schools of thought about the human mind and human psyche, and the therapeutic processes that would help people overcome fear, trauma, mental illness, and so forth? In the early days of psychotherapy, men were defining women, collectively and individually! Consequently, many of today's theories of psychology are the outcome of the very institutions that, in defining women, also abused them. Women were defined as unable to own property, hold high office, vote, or attend universities. Yet, men who were forming psychological schools of thought did so without even *addressing* these issues, or the fact that in defining women, men were verbally abusing them.

Of course, they could not see that what they were doing was wrong because they all agreed that it was right. Even though during the latter half of the nineteenth century and the beginning of the twentieth century some women were also researching, writing, and practicing psychotherapy, the larger male psychotherapeutic community ignored them. At that time, women were defined as not quite capable of doing what they were doing, in psychotherapy and in other fields. Men defined women in so many ways for so many generations that they did not find their own behavior irrational or strange, and they could not see the impact of their behavior on the women they were subsequently abusing. Although some women believed themselves to be exactly as they were defined, many did not.

It is no wonder that the people who developed the first schools of psychology ignored or were unconscious of the impact of verbal abuse on those subjected to it. How could they develop treatment for the abuser and the abused, if, for the most part, men who defined women developed the therapeutic practices? They defined women as not really real, or not really adequate, by excluding them from not only the psychotherapeutic community, but from most of the institutions they had established at that time. Let us look at a few examples to shed light on the context in which therapeutic practices began. In that light, we can clearly see why some therapists didn't, and to an extent still don't, learn about verbal abuse.

MEN DEFINE WOMEN IN ALL ASPECTS OF LIFE

As men developed laws regulating the ownership of land, the granting of deeds, and so forth, they defined women as incapable and unworthy of owning land. It wasn't until 1981 that the United States overturned a Louisiana state law designating a husband as "head and master" with unilateral control of property owned jointly with his wife.[4]

Women were also discouraged from attending colleges; they were banned from some colleges just because they were women. Oberlin College in Ohio became the first college to admit both men and women in 1833. In a general way, men confabulated reasons for their oppressive behavior, one being the general consensus that a lot of mental activity would negatively impact a young woman's health.

Despite Harvard University not granting a Ph.D. to psychologist Mary Whiton Calkin in 1896, in her forty-year career she made important contributions to the study of psychology. Fast-forward a century later, and we find an interesting contrast to the oppression of women, by those who defined them as unable to succeed in higher education: More women than men enrolled in the freshman class at Harvard in 2004. Further, media in both the United States and Canada reported that more women than men enrolled in college in both countries that year.[5]

As men developed political systems in the United States, they also defined women as not competent, or too ignorant, to vote. Not until the passage of the Nineteenth Amendment to the U.S. Constitution, in 1919, did women throughout the nation gain that right. And it wasn't until 1975 that the Supreme Court denied states the right to exclude women from juries.[6]

But the problem of some men not seeing women as real people did not end with the educational and political systems. In fact, for as long as people have been paid for work, women have been paid less than men for equal work, because men defined them as not quite as deserving. In 1963, however, there was an attempt to end this abuse in the United States when Congress passed the Equal Pay Act. As men formed corporate structures, they defined women as incapable of leading them. It wasn't until 1964 that the United States passed a law calling an end to this discrimination in employment based on both sex and race.[7] Sadly, however, over a couple's lifetime of equal work, the average woman will earn about $500,000 less than her mate; at the current rate of change, women will not receive equal pay until 2050.[8]

As men developed religious institutions, they defined women as unqualified to serve as ministers. It wasn't until the 1970s that some Christian religions began to ordain women. By 1975, the Anglican Church of Canada approved female ordination. And in 1976, the Episcopal Church in the United States opened up ordination of women as deacons, priests, or bishops. Similarly, women were ordained as rabbis since the early 1970s, eventually by all branches of Judaism except the Orthodox.

What we can see from these facts is that those who developed the early schools of psychology could hardly address *the defining of* women if they themselves defined women. The women who achieved, contributed, and forged their careers in a world of opposition did so with great determination in spite of the fact that the establishment did not encourage them.

The practice of therapy, the formation of the American Psychological Association (APA), and the publication of William

James's seminal work *Principles of Psychology* took place near the turn of the twentieth century. Between 1892 and 1902, many world-renowned leaders in psychology, including Sigmund Freud, Carl G. Jung, and Alfred Adler, published influential works. *Clearly, at the time that schools of psychology and methods of treatment were institutionalized, our culture was routinely abusing women by defining them in all aspects of their lives.* Defining people was not identified as a sickness, and no one could have imagined that *therapists* would need to know how to recognize verbal abuse and how to help people overcome it.

THE TIDES OF CHANGE

Now, because women fought to gain equal rights with men, many of the ways that men define women have changed. In many countries, men no longer define women as unable to own land, go to college, vote, be ministers, even be heads of state. But in other countries, abuse is still happening. In some cultures, the way women are defined and treated is horrifying. Men have formed religions or altered their own to teach that God has decreed that men "own" women, can tell them what to do and what they are. These men have institutionalized verbal abuse.

In the past, although women became very vocal about their situation—being paid less than men for the same work, having to take a back seat to men's privileged positions, and hitting the "glass ceiling" where they could rise no higher in the corporate world as they struggled to be treated with equality—they were hardly seen or heard. They wondered why so many men seemed unwilling to exchange ideas and thoughts with them, to express themselves to them, and to understand them. Some women thought that men were really afraid of women and their power to bring new life into the world. Or they thought that some men treated them unfairly in the workplace because men were afraid that the economy would collapse and that they would lose their incomes when women took their places. But what women did not realize was that besides these possible reasons, any man who ignored them did so because he saw them as dream women. He could not exchange ideas and thoughts with a real woman. He feared hearing and seeing her. If he did, he would lose his dream woman. The real woman would take her place and he would lose the rest of himself. Additionally, he sought to stay in the illusory state with his dream woman because she worked for him and produced for him, and accepted less than equal pay.

Men have continued to define women as if they were themselves living within the women they defined and so knew their inner reality and what they were capable of. It is because of this underlying abuse that women suffered all the rest and continue to suffer today. But even when many women come to the realization that men are defining them, they still wonder why.

After men developed governmental systems, why would they have defined women as incapable of voting?

After men instituted educational systems, why would they have defined women as inadequate and therefore to be excluded from colleges and universities?

Because they couldn't really see and hear the real woman.

And why was that?

Because they anchored their own feminine or undeveloped side in women and so couldn't see the real woman.

Why would they have an undeveloped side that they projected into women?

Because they couldn't develop the qualities *ascribed* to the feminine gender within themselves.

Why couldn't they develop all their qualities?

Because they disparaged qualities and functions, like feeling and intuition.

And why was that?

Because their fathers and their culture disparaged these qualities.

But why would their fathers disparage these important aspects of their own sons?

Because they wanted to make them into "real men," that is, unfeeling, insensitive, non-nurturing, and basically unconscious, robotic soldiers.

And why was that?

So they wouldn't feel and thus, suffer in war.

But what about verbally abusive women? Were they trained not to feel, in order to be like soldiers? Of course verbally abusive women also define their spouse's inner world, or very being, but they do not become disconnected from themselves because of a training system handed down from mother to daughter, as described above. Instead, they become disconnected from themselves and develop a dream spouse, for the most part, because they were severely neglected or traumatized. This may be why I have never seen a woman change from verbally abusing her spouse to treating him with kindness and empathy. They are too damaged.

GUIDELINES FOR COUNSELING

The questions and answers above explain how otherwise rational men can define someone's inner world, their very being. Some therapists don't know what is behind the verbally abusive man's behavior. Since the whole paradigm of the dream woman is relatively new to therapists, many partners of verbally abusive men have told me that their therapists thought that they somehow caused their spouse's behavior.

A woman who is with a batterer can call 911 when she is hit, and pursue justice in the legal system. If it is reliable, it will eventfully get her batterer into jail and/or an anger management program and may possibly wake him up to further help. If she is not hit, however, but is verbally abused, she has to find a way by herself or with some agency or counselor or church member to reach her abuser and get him to see what he is doing. If this problem is not dealt with, she may go through the difficult changes involved with leaving him, but the verbally abusive man will be the same with his next partner.

Many women who come to me for help have been the targets of tirades or subtle ongoing definitions of themselves; they have suffered abuse that wore away all their resolve and sense of self—like a stream wearing away the earth to leave the abyss, the grand canyon, the emptiness of their knowing there was so little left of themselves that they would soon die—yet were unable to define or name the problem. They despaired of stopping it from happening. They walked on eggshells, so to speak, just to survive some nameless torment that told them there was something wrong with them. But when they said, "I can't take any more," their mates would say, "If there is a problem then it's a two-way street." As one abuser said, "I will never talk to a therapist unless you agree that the problems in our relationship are a fifty-fifty thing. You are as responsible as I am."

And their counselors often said the same.

The verbally abusive man will usually go with his partner to see a counselor, but only because he is aggravated that his partner will "never be happy" or "never give up complaining" until he does. However, the usual experience of seeing a counselor is very disappointing, as we've seen. One of the problems that isn't usually addressed or sometimes even recognized is that verbal abuse takes place in the so-called safe space of a counselor's office. Here is an example.

A woman I'll call Sheila said that her husband was, and still is, very open to counseling. However, he always tells the counselors how Sheila is the cause of all their problems, and the counselors tend to believe him. "He is usually very charming," she said. "I really need a counselor with knowledge in the arena of verbal abuse."

Yes, I agreed, she would need a counselor who could spot verbal abuse. Typically, I ask my clients, "What did you hear?" In this case, I asked Sheila, "How did your husband define you as the problem to the therapist?" She described a typical scenario. At the counselor's office, where both husband and wife are present, the husband says, "I really love my wife so much; she is just wonderful and we are usually really happy together."

He smiles at her, then, turning toward the therapist, speaks sincerely and a bit sadly. "But sometimes it is kind of hard for me, because she blows things out of proportion, and I don't know what to do to get things back on course. Do you think we just need a vacation, with how busy we are? We don't have a lot of time for fun."

Here the counselor has an opportunity to stop the verbally abusive statement, "She blows things out of proportion," and to say something like a little intervention: "Excuse me. I have to interrupt here. What seems to be the underlying problem is that I heard you say your partner 'blows things out of proportion.' Do you know that statement defines her inner world, judges her perceptions, discounts and denies her experience, assaults her mind and consciousness, and likely leaves her feeling unseen and unheard, as if she has no relationship—even when you didn't mean for her to have a disturbing experience?"

The counselor might continue: "So, instead, would you please simply ask her what has really bothered her lately? And, would you also ask her if she thinks that you're usually happy together?"

By the counselor's intervention—even if it is not particularly instructive but is as simple as, "Did you hear how you just defined your partner?"—verbal abuse is addressed, and the abuser's behavior is brought to his awareness. And, certainly, the partner does not have to face a more abusive spouse whose position is tacitly approved by a silent counselor.

Since the problem of counselors not recognizing and stopping verbal abuse in counseling sessions is so widespread, I've recommended that clients who are already in couples counseling use a basic Counseling Guidelines form that I have created for their own safety. Although I don't recommend couples counseling that bases responsibility for the relationship on a fifty-fifty model, if you want to get your abuser to a counselor, you can take the Counseling Guidelines, found on page 71, with you. It proposes that the counselor agree to intervene if anyone is defined or characterized during the counseling session and the partner is too traumatized or too brainwashed to respond. The response could be as sample as, "What I heard you say, that your wife 'blows things out of proportion,' is not okay. Do you know why?" Or it could include some of the information from Sheila's potential intervention. If you, your spouse, and the counselor cannot agree to it, then why go to the session where verbal abuse is allowed to take place? It is truly a nightmare for anyone to go to a counselor or any authority with their spouse only to experience abuse that is not addressed immediately in the session.

I recommend that any therapist who has a couple coming in for counseling propose that the couple read and initial the Counseling Guidelines to ensure that the counseling session takes place in a safe environment. No verbal abuse is allowed to pass by unaddressed by the abused person—or, if that doesn't happen, by the counselor. Even if a couple is coming in to discuss money issues, or whether or not to move to a larger home, or for some addiction like gambling, the possibility exists that their presenting issue is not the core problem. If the therapist hears one person defining the other, then she or he is hearing verbal abuse and it is not safe for the couple to meet together. Coming in separately may be helpful instead.

At least half the women I consult have seen a counselor at some time and usually with their spouse, hoping that the counselor will spot the abuse, help the spouse to see what he is doing, and resolve it. Usually, a woman goes with the knowledge that her abuser has already determined that it is *her* problem. And sometimes she goes with the thought that maybe there is something wrong with her. She is at her most vulnerable. However, I have never seen abuse to be a fifty-fifty thing. For that reason I have developed the following set of Counseling Guidelines to ensure that verbal abuse is not tacitly approved in the counseling session.

Counseling Guidelines

In the interests of promoting mutual respect and clear communications, these guidelines are designed to assure everyone that no one in this session will be defined or characterized by anyone else.

Neither of us wants to hear verbal abuse, the defining or characterization of another person, at any time, and especially in a therapeutic setting that is meant for healing and awareness. Therefore, we agree to meet here with the intention that neither one of us covertly or overtly defines or characterizes the other.

1. We agree to say, "What did you say?" if we are defined or characterized by the other.
2. We agree not to interrupt the other, except if we are defined or characterized by the other, and to say, "What did you say?" if that occurs.
3. In any other case, if one person interrupts the other, the interrupted person will raise their hand in a "stop" gesture, or if he or she is too traumatized, or shocked, or too used to being interrupted, or too afraid to object, the counselor agrees to intercede, holding up his or her hand, and saying, "stop" or "hold it."

4. The counselor supports us in achieving mutual freedom from verbal abuse by interceding when she or he witnesses it. This might be achieved in the following way:

 a. If anyone defines or characterizes the other and the person who is defined or characterized is too traumatized, or shocked, or too used to, or adapted to that behavior to stop it, the counselor will interrupt the speaker by saying "What?" or, "What did you say?"

 b. If the person who is asked what they just said can't recall what they just said, the counselor will remind him or her by saying, "I heard you say . . . Is that what you meant?"

 c. The speaker agrees to rephrase what he or she said. For example, "That came out wrong. What I meant to say is . . ." so that it isn't defining or characterizing of the other. The speaker may ask the counselor for help in understanding how what was said defined or characterized the other person or may ask the counselor for an idea of how to rephrase the comment.

 d. At no time will anyone say, "You're attacking me," because that gives the accused person no understanding, and defines his or her motives and intentions. For example, a person may say, "I felt hurt when I heard . . ." and the other person, instead of feeling concern or remorse or empathy, might respond, "I don't need to be attacked like that," or, "You're attacking me."

The definitions and examples below are meant to clarify the terms in this Agreement, as they may have completely different meanings for different people.

Definitions

Attack: to abuse

Abuse: to define or characterize

Examples

- Things that define: "You always..." "You're... " "I don't see why you..." "She just wants..."
- Things that characterize: "You've brought a bag of grenades." This characterizes the other person as the enemy, ready for attack. In actuality, a person so characterized had brought a small bag of books to a meeting.

The "grenades" example used in the Guidelines illustrates the heartbreak of verbal abuse. A partner who wants love is instead frustrated and made crazy because she cannot get her mate to see that she is not the enemy. In this case, that she is not there with something to attack him, be it real or metaphor.

You're attacking me is one of the most crazy-making statements a person can make. If the partner is not in fact assaulting her mate but is trying to find solutions, her heart can break over the accusation. This is chiefly because the accusation shows her how futile her efforts are.

Abusive behaviors can slip right by anyone at some time. Not long ago an auto commercial showed a couple in an attractive car. The man was driving. He approached a puddle of water in the road and right in the middle of his partner's conversation with him, he stopped the car and jumped out while she sat in the car with a startled and confused expression on her face. Meanwhile, he lay his jacket down over the puddle to obviously protect the car. As he got back in she said, "Why don't you do that for me?" And he said, "Do what?"

Walking away when people are talking to us and pretending that what just happened didn't happen, may be quaint in a commercial, but these defining behaviors (like you aren't there, and what you perceive isn't real) embody the defining and denial that the partners of verbal abusers face daily. I believe the goal is that we become conscious of the respect due to human beings and stop abuse when we hear or see it. Who wants to buy that car?

One last word: We need all counselors, therapists, and leaders to know about verbal abuse so that people can get the help they need when they need it.

5

IS CHANGE POSSIBLE?

DURING THE LAST HUNDRED YEARS, women in the United States and Western countries have been less and less defined as inadequate, incapable, or unequal to men because they have fought for equal rights. Although the Equal Rights Amendment to the United States Constitution is not yet ratified, judicial rulings and new legislation have given women many of the rights that were previously withheld from them. They have the right to vote and to own property, and women now hold many positions from which they were excluded in the past. Sexual harassment is now against the law and those who violate it are subject to prosecution.

It is interesting to note that in less than a hundred years, the United States has gone from denying half of its citizens the right to vote—defining them as incapable or worse—to fighting a war thousands of miles away to gain the citizens there the right to vote.

We are far from a functional society. Although women are generally less often defined—that is, verbally abused—in public arenas, unfortunately, many are still defined in their homes. We know that verbal abuse precedes all domestic violence. In the United States, about 4,000 women a year are killed by their husbands or boyfriends, ex-husbands or ex-boyfriends.

If we had a healthy world—and most important, healthy leaders—people would speak truthfully, motivated by their desire to be real, honest, and rational. Their motive to change, from defining women to respecting them, would go beyond the fear of criminal prosecution. But hate crimes still occur, and domestic violence is definitely a hate crime.

Yet, there are positives in the socio-political-economic systems in which we live, in communities, states, countries, and coalitions. In many ways, change is going on all the time. All the therapies, counseling strategies, anger management programs, twelve-step programs, checklists, and advice columns that permeate our culture are meant to bring about change. And they are highly effective when they address a core problem; the agoraphobic finally leaves the house happily, the alcoholic stops drinking, and the parent learns how to encourage good behavior. But all the talk and all the support groups in the world cannot bring about change when the problem remains hidden.

To create change in the age-old problem of verbal abuse, I believe we must have a clear recognition of the core problem, that is, the fact that the verbally abusive man appears to live in his partner via his dream woman, rather than stay alone in his own body. In so doing, he does not feel crazy or irrational when he tells her what she is, should do, and so forth, as if he were she. (See Appendix A, page 227, for examples.)

Fortunately, a change has already begun. Men have been speaking out in recent years against verbal abuse, recognizing it as a part of domestic violence.

Change from verbally abusive behaviors to validating ones is possible in many cases. Later in this chapter, I list the many factors that go against change as well as those that suggest that change might be possible. It is highly unlikely, if not impossible, for some people to change—for instance, people with personality disorders (borderline, narcissistic, antisocial). They can't relate to others in a healthy way. It is as if they have a skewed view of the world, or of other people, and are misconnected or hardwired wrong. A woman who is with a verbally abusive man who has a personality disorder has a much more difficult road ahead of her.

Another type of man who is less likely to change is one who is physically violent, threatens a woman's life, or tells her he has a right to control her or be in charge of her. Even presenting a man like this with the Agreement could be dangerous. Although the Agreement is designed to wake up a verbally abusive man, a man who believes that he has a right to control another human being, and to punish her if she does not conform to his will, already knows what he is doing and thinks it is okay.

COMMON QUESTIONS ABOUT CHANGE

Having heard from many thousands of people, I want to share with you two of the most common questions that women have asked about change.

1. Have you seen verbally abusive men change?

I have seen some men change from being verbally abusive to validating and expressing empathy to their partners. I believe that verbally abusive men, who want to change more than anything else and who commit to and do the necessary work, have a strong chance of changing. Change has already begun in a broader sense, as women are seen and heard in more places than before.

At one time, the only domestic abuse that was recognized was physical. And, until recently, most men who indulged in verbal abuse knew neither why they were abusive, nor, often, *that* they were abusing. As one man said,

"I truly believed that I was the poster child of *what* to be as a parent and partner in a relationship. Was I ever wrong! Although I have never hit a woman or child, as I know how defenseless both are against a raging lunatic, I surely am one verbally abusive s.o.b."

As unable as this man had been to see himself, he actually woke up to the reality of his abusive behavior when he understood that he had tried to shape his partner in his dream woman. He was now ready to begin the work of actual change in order that he might truly see and hear his partner. Men who, above all things, want to change, and who get properly focused therapy, and who do the reading and exercises I suggest, can often change. Whether their partners will want to stay with them usually depends on how traumatized they are. Some partners deem it wise to keep an eye on their mate as he does the work of changing, rather than to keep an eye on someone new, of whom they know little.

More Likely to Change

- He is more likely to change if he has actualized himself to some degree in the world. For instance, he is able to keep a steady job, earn a living, support his family.
- He is more likely to change if he hasn't indulged in violent behaviors.
- He is more likely to change if he doesn't threaten to take the children away from his partner should she choose to end the relationship.

- He is more likely to change if he has an honest character. For instance, he has never been convicted of a crime or engaged in fraudulent activities.
- He is more likely to change if he doesn't pursue other women.
- He is most likely to change if he agrees to the Agreement and to do the recommended steps for change.

2. How would I know that the man I love has what it takes to change?

A person with a steady job, who has no severe escapist habits, would be more likely to change than one who avoids reality. If he is the type of person who comes home every night, takes care of things around the house, talks to his children once in a while, but is irritable and verbally abusive at times, he is more likely to want to change. But this can happen only if he comes to the realization that he has been defining his partner—and if he doesn't want to start over with a new relationship and possibly half of his assets. Considering these possibilities and the loss of an intact family, he may be motivated to attend to the relationship and whatever it is that is bothering his wife. Other motives come later.

He is unlikely to change and may be dangerous to even be around if he has violent or threatening behaviors and, most important, the partner's intuition tells her to escape.

Less Likely to Change

Can he change if he has some of the following behaviors? The more he has the less likely he is to change. If he has affairs and also some of the other characteristics and behaviors listed on page 80, it is highly unlikely that he will change. He has already lined up another body for his dream woman, if he can't keep the one he's got.

- He is less likely to change if he has nothing to lose financially when the relationship ends.
- He is less likely to change if he has behaviors that keep him from facing himself. For instance, he is an active alcoholic or drug addict.
- He is less likely to change if he has compulsive disorders. For instance, he escapes reality in compulsive gambling or spending.
- He is less likely to change if he has been diagnosed as having a personality disorder.
- He is less likely to change if he has had affairs during marriage or a committed relationship.
- He is less likely to change if he has a history of physical violence.
- He is less likely to change if he has no friends or emotional connections with anyone.
- He is less likely to change if he is verbally abusive before marriage.
- He is even less likely to change if he is verbally abusive before living with the partner.
- He is less likely to change if he consistently blames others for any problem in his life.
- He is less likely to change if he periodically demonstrates violence.
- He is less likely to change if he plays with weapons.
- He is less likely to change if he mistreats animals.
- He is less likely to change if he teasingly torments a child.
- He is less likely to change if he has said, "I won't change."
- He is less likely to change if his culture gives him permission to dominate other human beings.

Not Likely to Change but Worth a Try

If, from the previous lists, you see that he is unlikely to change, it may still be worthwhile to compose the Agreement. How to prepare for it, present it, and write it are all explained in Chapters 8, 9, and 10, respectively. Although you may be planning to leave, if he sees it, he might become a bit more aware of his abuse of you. If this is the case, he may be less inclined to retaliate against you for your choice to leave. In any case, composing the Agreement and presenting it can usually be done in a few days' time; it is certainly worth pursuing if you want to see whether he can begin the process of change. All this should be done with the knowledge that it will not change him. It will simply be the first time he may notice that he has been defining his partner's inner reality, and therefore has been acting irrationally. This could motivate him to change or to be less vindictive.

Whether he is likely or unlikely to want to change, you will not know until he not only receives the Agreement, but also hears your responses to his behavior and begins to question his own behavior. Almost all men who verbally abuse their partners believe that they are not abusive, that whatever discord occurs is just part of the "ups and downs" in relationships, or is his partner's fault and, surprisingly, that *she* has a lot of the power.

There is, however, always the man who will not change and the most evident is the one who says, "I won't change." Shockingly, even when some men realize that they have harmed someone, they may choose not to change. The following case serves to illustrate this.

This is the story of a man who verbally abused both his wife and his daughter for some time before he became physically abusive. His adult daughter, whom I'll call Beth, said that he presented himself to the world as an "upstanding guy." He could be a good neighbor to anyone or even hold public trust. She said, "He comes across as a great guy, volunteers for everything. He smiles all the time, shakes everyone's hand, wears custom-tailored suits, and even uses hairspray. He has a perfect persona."

Beth went on to tell me that while she was growing up, he told everyone outside of their home how great his daughter was and how proud he was of her.

Ironically, it wasn't until after the Child Abuse Prevention and Treatment Act came into effect in 1974 that he added physical abuse to his verbal abuse, yet no one availed himself or herself of this law to act on Beth's behalf. Unfortunately, when his daughter came to school with a bruised and lacerated face, no teacher asked, "How did that happen?"

When she was old enough to sort it all out, she told him she wanted change. She reminded him of her childhood with him and his behavior even after she reached adulthood. She said, "When I confronted him about his horrible abuse of me, he said, 'I know what I am doing is wrong but I *will not* change my behavior at all.'"

Although his wife had divorced him because of his behavior, he presents himself as an expert on relationships. Beth determined to protect her own children from him, and she has. This man has five grandchildren he has never met. I want to emphasize here that the defining abuse of people usually takes place behind closed doors and that I am always amazed at how prevalent it is. At the same time, I believe that many people are *not* like Beth's father. Although they have managed to get through life disregarding others, once they realize that they are harming those closest to them, they want to change.

6

THE PARTNER WANTS HIM TO CHANGE

EVEN WHEN FEELING LIKE THEY are going crazy in a relationship that just isn't working, even when they are being verbally abused in some senseless game that their spouses seem to be playing, one with changing rules and no real winner, many women wonder if their mate can change. You might be wondering it, too.

Here is how one woman described the way her husband treated her and how she hopes he may wake up and stop his verbally abusive behavior. I found her letter particularly compelling, and she kindly gave me permission to use it in this book. I believe that she has found her voice—a voice that will resonate with many readers.

"My life never made sense. I couldn't tell if I was coming or going, and I'm a very successful professional with a good career.

I have always been a strong person, but all that changed before I knew it. I began to doubt myself. The brainwashing was constant, subtle, and pervasive. All of my awareness, energy, passions, views, perspectives, were like beams of light absorbed into a black hole. Not the tiniest glimmer of me was reflected back to me. And any glimmer bright enough to last a few seconds was doused by his cold, cutting comments and his vile behavior.

"Yet it was all so indescribable. I hardly knew why just being, just existing, was so exhausting. Then finally I woke up to the craziness of it all. Like a crack in the cosmos, a glimmer of light came to me. A glimmer came to me and all the pieces fit. His behaviors toward me were all in some way defining of me and so were, of course, totally irrational. Now, believe it or not, it was not the cursing or the spitting in my face, but it was that he told me, 'The problem with you is, you're so fuckin' stupid! You're a loser!' Well, I always thought he could think I'm a bitch or not there for him, but I absolutely knew I *wasn't* 'stupid.' Isn't that funny? Some little word like *stupid* finally woke me up.

"Now, I really do want to exhaust all options for the success of our family before I choose divorce."

As a woman's relationship becomes more difficult, she usually wants the man she is with to be nice again, just like he was before he anchored his dream woman in her.

TO STAY OR TO GO

Women in marriages and long-term relationships who have been with abusive men want to see them change; unless, that is, they are so traumatized they are certain they'll never feel safe and protected with them again; unless they have lost all trust because of the verbal deception. As one woman said, "He's always telling me what I am and what I'm thinking, just as if he was me, and I always thought I could explain it to him, one last time, and he would get it. But now I know how deeply he deceives himself and how constantly and unconsciously he has attempted to deceive me." They want to see him change unless they are so hurt, they really don't care whether he changes—in which case, they just don't want to see him again. And, of course, they want to see change unless they fear for their lives, because they have been threatened or terrified by his verbal violence. If they do feel threatened or their intuition tells them that they are in danger, it is imperative that they get help, make a plan, and leave.

It is important for you to recognize how you feel around a husband or boyfriend who loses his temper, ignores you, and/or puts you down. And it is important for you to recognize when you are traumatized. After an encounter with a verbally abusive mate, you may feel stirred up inside, upset, unable to focus and unable to feel like yourself for several days; you may describe it as having a "setback." This is what trauma is.

If you plan to leave your abuser, you may decide to present the Agreement anyway, slightly modified so that it is more a statement than an Agreement. Or, you may choose to leave a modified version on the kitchen counter, in his mailbox, or on his e-mail for him to find after you are gone. This will help him to understand why you have left. If he had been able to hear you during the relationship, he would already know why you're leaving. But this is not usually the case.

If you want to change, it could be for many reasons. It would be so much easier if he just would, so much less painful, so much less traumatic. You are constantly trying to stabilize the relationship that he ends and reconstitutes so frequently. And most likely, more than anything, you want your relationship to feel like a relationship, that is, an open exchange between two people.

No matter how much a man changes from indulging in verbal abuse to being supportive and validating, a woman who is traumatized may always feel re-traumatized in his presence. This depends on how long she was traumatized, how much support she has, how crazy-making the abuse was, and many other factors. Every battered woman whom I have spoken with, as well as those I've heard about from leaders of support groups, who knows what verbal abuse is has said that verbal abuse is worse, lasts longer, and is harder to recover from than physical abuse. (Though that might not be the case if a physical assault is severe or permanently damaging.)

While you may want him to change, you may at the same time be planning to leave if he doesn't. If you are thinking of leaving your mate, you must consider many things: if you can stay where you are; where you will go if you can't; what will least disrupt your family's lives; if you will need a job or two jobs; what car you will have; and where your support system will be. And these are just a *few* of your considerations. All are part of your open-ended and unpredictable future. And, like many women, you may face the threat of losing your children.

Hundreds of documented cases reveal that evaluators and judges have given full legal and physical custody to fathers. Many of these fathers have histories of domestic violence; some have been incestuous. In some states, however, if a child who's nine or ten years old talks about sexual abuse by the father, the mother is often attacked—first by the father of the children, then the courts—and is accused of alienating the child from the father. The mothers, who were loving primary caregivers, then lose custody. Some haven't seen their children in years. They just didn't have the hundreds of thousands of dollars needed to defend themselves from false accusations. Their soon-to-be-ex or ex-husbands did. (Turn to Appendix E, page 255, for places to turn to for help and information.)

Leaving isn't a first choice for many women, however. The partner loved him enough to marry him. She wants the marriage to last her lifetime. She fears that if she leaves, her children will be unprotected in her absence. The partner who is hoping for an improvement in her relationship wants him to be nice again, the way he was when they met and when they were dating, before he switched, before he anchored his dream woman in her. She wants the warmth and kindness and the feeling that someone is there for her, cares for her, wants to share his life with her.

Without a doubt, this partner would prefer to get back the man she knew when they were courting, rather than leave the man he became. She would prefer that he change rather than that she leave her home, her social life, time with their children, and possibly her economic security and all that she had tried to create. This partner wants to give it her best shot, so to speak, to know she's done every last thing she can think of to make the relationship work. She wants to find out, finally, whether change is possible. She never dreamt this could happen to her. She'd always believed that if she did her part, did everything possible to make her relationship work, it would.

HIS CHANGE SEEMS REAL

The partner who hopes for a change for the better in her relationship often wonders how long change would take. How long would it take for her verbally abusive mate to become normal, that is, a kind person who is kind to her? Real change is not achieved by an act of will on the part of the verbally abusive person. Change takes time and depends on how dedicated the verbally abusive man is to achieving that goal. Although awareness and the desire to change can make a real difference in the verbally abusive man's behavior, these are simply prerequisites to change.

If the man who has been verbally abusing his partner comes home to find her gone, he may be so overwhelmed with loss that he will say or do anything to get her back. After all, she embodied his dream woman. No doubt, when he says he has changed *he will sound perfectly sincere.* And he might, indeed, pass a lie detector test while swearing that he will never do it again. This is because he really does see his partner in a new way. Just as he had anchored his dream woman in her when he felt very secure, conversely, he withdraws his dream woman when he feels less secure. If his unconscious could speak, it might say something like, "This body *might leave me* now. It's no longer a safe harbor for my dream woman."

With his dream woman withdrawn, he once again sees his partner through the vision of his dream woman—right before his eyes—as if with rose-colored glasses. His partner looks better than before. He wants her back because, to him, she is everything he ever wanted, the rest of himself. He begins courting her again.

This is why the cycle of violence occurs. Anger management groups and domestic violence prevention agencies are so aware of the cycle of violence that they usually provide newcomers with a circular chart diagramming the cycle. It goes like this:

1. *The Honeymoon Stage:* He is courting her to win her back.
2. *The Tension-Building Stage:* He is becoming irritated and angry with his partner while managing his anger.
3. *The Explosion:* He becomes verbally and/or physically abusive.

Although the cycle seems as old as time, and so, somehow an inevitable part of the human psyche, it is not inevitable. Now, for the first time, we know precisely what the cycle is about, why the cycle repeats as it does, and why the shift from abusive to courting behavior takes place in some relationships.

It is not that the abuser builds up steam as if he were a pressure cooker; instead, it is that as soon as his partner comes back to him, hoping he is dedicated to change, he feels secure: "This body *has chosen* me now." So, he anchors his dream woman in her, deeper than ever before. From that moment on, he can neither see nor hear the real woman again. Like some great gothic and mysterious myth, the ritual is complete, the spell is cast, and the honeymoon is over. When the real woman starts showing up where the dream woman is supposed to be, he growls, frowns, mocks, gives her warning signs to silence her. His anger grows. He tries to manage his anger, then he can no longer stand it. The real woman insists on showing up, and he explodes. His unconscious screams, "Where did my dream woman go? Where did the rest of me go? Yikes, I'm being killed—severed from myself!"

Some women say something along the lines of, "It seems like they want to get back at you all the time for existing." When I hear this I tell them that this depends how deeply anchored they are in their partner and how large the dream woman is— large, not in physical terms, but in psychological ones; that is, how much of the verbally abusive man is lost in his unconscious, feeding and filling out his dream woman.

The more deeply he has anchored this dream woman in his partner, and the "bigger" his dream woman is—in other words, the larger his unlived, unintegrated self is—the more his partner's realness or authenticity is an assault on his connection to reality, even on his existence as he knows it.

THE DREAM WOMAN IS HIS REALITY

I am emphasizing the dream woman because, without knowing about her, the partner may try to bring change in futile ways.

The partner of an abuser can be stuck for years trying to change herself so the relationship will improve. She may search for answers, read everything, try everything until she knows what is wrong, and ultimately realizes that changes in her behavior will not change him. This is true, even if she has been told by an authority figure, "If you change, he'll change." Such a declaration is nonsense. His problems originated when he was very young; they may, in the most rare instances, even be genetically influenced (see page 44). The only possible way to bring change, outside of some miraculously unusual awakening or deeply spiritual transformation, is by demanding conscious, real, sane behavior that allows the verbally abusive man to see that his partner is very tired of watching him pretend to be her, a woman.

Since many women are not sure what is happening to them when they are defined in a constant, sometimes subtle way, they have no idea what to do. They may face anger, accusation, and blame so constantly that they think they are doing something wrong. They become so focused on saying things "right" so as not to anger their mate, that they cannot see that it is not actually their fault.

The Agreement has helped many men to see what they are doing, how they have attempted to silence the real woman, how controlling and desperate their behavior is, and it gives them their first glimmer—indeed, their very first hint—that they have attempted to *be* their partners.

Usually when a woman meets a man who may ultimately try to control her through verbal abuse, she sees only his outside-world persona. He still sees her as part of the world, beyond himself, on the outside, where his persona was perfected. While he courted her, trying to win her over, he presented his perfected persona and seemed to be wonderful. But when he switched, she was essentially his dream woman, and from that moment on, he could no longer bear to see or hear the real woman.

If others do not see it and there is no one to explain it to her, the partner experiences confusion and even a sense of unreality. Without outside intervention, new knowledge, or wise input, she has no way to orient to *actual* reality. Looking back on her experience, one woman said, "My reality was not reality, so I questioned everything: every choice I'd made and how I could be in this situation. I didn't know about Dream Woman so there was no way to explain, even to myself, what was happening and why it was happening. There is no way to describe the experience."

If we go back for a moment to the time when men defined women as unsuitable for higher education, we can see the futility of a woman trying to be "some way" so he will stop defining her. We know that no matter how the young women acted, no matter how they changed, the men who defined them would still define them in the same way. They had to get a law passed for equal education in order *not* to be defined as unsuitable for higher education.

Women want change to end their pain, to protect their children, to have kindness back in their relationships, to keep their families intact, to not have to start over again, to not have to go through the greatest change in their lives when they are exhausted and often ill from verbal abuse. The mental anguish and emotional pain that verbal abuse generates cannot be over-emphasized.

There are endless other reasons that a woman wants her significant other or spouse to wake up to his behavior and to change from indulging in verbal abuse to offering validation and respect of her experiences, her views, and her true self.

When women hear their inner realities defined, they know that they are not seen and heard for who they are. So, of course, they want the verbally abusive man to change. But if she can't find ways to bring change, and if she is told that she has no right to ask for change because she is "too sensitive," she ends up traumatized. She hears that her inner pain and self-perceptions are wrong. She is not seen or heard, and since deep in her soul she has a special awareness that consciousness itself comes from the Divine, that level of consciousness is also assaulted. She experiences something like "God" being slapped in the face within her. Although her relationship is ended, there is no funeral at which she can display her grief or anyone bringing casseroles to ease her pain. She may harbor the fear of being crazy. She searches for ways to not make it be some fault that she has overlooked. Her mental anguish is so great she becomes exhausted and suffers from panic attacks or anxiety. Her exhaustion increases as she struggles to maintain her own perceptions and her own experiences in the face of their being denied.

People who are severely traumatized feel as if they are never going to feel okay. For them, it is like they were prisoners of war, terribly mistreated, and living with the prison guard. Some men are motivated to change as they realize that this is the impact of their behavior, but many do not come to that realization easily. Let us look now at some of the prime forces that motivate a man to change from verbally abusing his partner to treating her with kindness and respect.

7

WHAT MOTIVATES HIM TO CHANGE?

THERE ARE MANY MOTIVES FOR a man to change from verbally abusive behavior to kind and understanding behavior. We know that one of his greatest needs is to keep his dream woman alive and well in his partner's body. In fact, this is why he defines her in the first place. He wants to shape her into his dream woman. Therefore, not losing the body that harbors her is of prime importance and becomes his primary motive. Once he comes to the realization that his partner could leave, however, he may begin to look more closely at his behavior and consequently find many other motives to change. However, there are exceptions that lessen his motivation or block it entirely. Let's look at some of these possibilities.

HE WANTS TO KEEP THE BODY THAT HARBORS HIS DREAM WOMAN

If his psychological survival depends on his keeping his dream woman alive in his partner's body, as indeed it seems to, then it would follow that knowing where his dream woman was and knowing he had access to her would be his most pressing need. A verbally abusive man may experience anxiety, even panic, when he doesn't know where she is. He may feel suicidal if she has left, or he may become anxious or very angry if he thinks she might leave. In many cases, if she leaves he will stalk her. On rare but tragically real occasions, he may even try to intimidate or kill the people who stand in the way of his access to the body that harbors his dream woman.

It follows that his most pressing motive to change would be to ensure that he keeps his partner or that he gets her back. In most cases, he wants to do whatever is necessary to achieve this. And, having no idea at this stage what the problem really is, he thinks that gifts and "I love yous" will achieve his goal. He may know that he has been "rough" on her, but thinks that now he'll be better.

Some abusers, rather than trying to understand their partners and what they have been doing to them instead threaten them in an attempt to keep them present. The first or most common threat is that they will take away the children if the partners leave. In many cases, they can make good on this threat if they have the money for court and other related costs. Other threats are of suicide ("I'll kill myself if you leave me.") or of murder ("I'll kill you if you leave me."). If you hear these threats, you should immediately share this information with as many people as possible, including a domestic violence prevention agency, the authorities, and an attorney.

The Exception

The exception is if he has moved his dream woman to another body by having an affair, or if he has splintered her into many other bodies by having multiple simultaneous affairs. Then, of course, he has no need to get back his partner and so it is highly unlikely that he will change. Even if he relinquishes all others and says there will be no more, he has already shown that he is adept at moving his dream woman from one body to another.

HE DOESN'T WANT TO DIVIDE ASSETS

When the man who indulges in verbal abuse realizes that he may lose both his wife and her assets, which are community property and which till then he likely considered his, he will usually feel motivated to make some change or to do something, like couple's counseling, to ensure that she stay. These men then present their perfected persona to the counselor to convince the counselor and the partner that she is expecting too much.

If the partner does decide to leave, she may naively think that her mate will be fair—and he might be, *if* he understands that he forced her to go because of his abusive behavior. But if he hasn't seen the Agreement and doesn't comprehend that he drove her away, he may be very angry that she is leaving him.

The Exception

Often, the verbally abusive man will try to hide all mutual funds earned during the marriage, even to pull money out of the equity in their home and to hide it before she realizes what he is doing. Of course, the only way she can then have her financial share is to file for divorce and have a forensic accountant find her money. He may threaten to break her financially. Like many controlling men, he may think that if his partner stayed home raising children, even home schooling them, she did "nothing." He earned money and she didn't, so she doesn't deserve her share of their joint assets. He might not even consider that she's not likely to "catch up" the years she gave up while she supported him in building his career and/or caring for their children.

HE WANTS TO PROTECT HIS NICE GUY IMAGE

The verbally abusive man usually sees himself as a good guy and really believes that he is. He may depend on his image in his career, and with family and friends. Certainly, he wants to be seen as able to keep his partner, rather than be left by her. Usually his view of himself as a nice guy begins to change when he sees the Agreement. He may wake up in some other way, too, but once awake, he may be more motivated to change.

The Exception

Since he feels provoked by his partner's separate thoughts, actions, etc., he thinks that she is the cause of problems in the relationship. He is closed to any alternative perspective, so he characterizes her to family, friends, and the community as a bad wife and mother. He keeps his image while trying to destroy her credibility.

HE WANTS TO KEEP HIS FAMILY INTACT

If he sees himself as a family man, he will usually want to continue life as it has been. If his children are young, he doesn't usually want to spend his time being a full-time caretaker on the days he would have visitation with them. The whole idea of this dramatic life change may motivate him to find out what is "bothering" his wife.

The Exception

If his partner does leave permanently, he may try to take the children away 100 percent of the time to "get back" at her. This is a very common pattern. Possibly, if he sees the Agreement, it will give her some time and he won't be so vindictive. If she has already left, it will be a statement of why. Many men feel shocked when their partners leave, thinking there have just been "a few fights."

HE DOESN'T WANT WOMEN TO KEEP LEAVING HIM

If other women have left him, he realizes that possibly the pattern will repeat itself. The past will, in fact, predict the future if he doesn't find out what is wrong, why women leave him, why he feels angry so often, just what his partner has been trying to tell him, or what it is she wants him to change. So he decides to listen, and he cannot avoid hearing the Agreement.

The Exception

He decides women leave men because they are evil, unpredictable, crazy, or whatever suits him at the moment to justify one more woman leaving him.

HE DOESN'T WANT TO BE IRRATIONAL

Since he isn't his partner and doesn't know what she is, thinks, is trying to do, etc., telling her that he does know is very irrational.

Coming to this realization, he wants to change. He had always thought that he was rational and she wasn't.

The Exception

He is so angry that he says she makes him say all these things, irrational or not; he doesn't care and he is not responsible. He says that he is always rational—except when *she* drives him to say irrational things. Speaking irrationally, he says, "You made me do this." No one can "make" another person do or say something. The partner doesn't live within him, so she cannot make him do what he does.

Since he thinks all those close to him are of one mind—his— he has difficulty discerning the difference between what he says to his partner and what she says to him. Jailed batterers almost universally believe that their being in prison is their wives' fault.

HE DOESN'T WANT TO FEEL OR BE SEEN AS AFRAID

He realizes that he has great difficulty seeing his partner as a separate person and that he fears her separateness and her freedom to be her own person. He is intelligent and knows enough to understand that he needs real therapeutic help to develop a center within himself so that he won't be centered in his partner. He wants to stand on his two feet, stay in his own space, and not invade hers. He knows he cannot use his backward connection to her to stave off his underlying anxiety and feelings of emptiness. He knows he has been living in a dream world, or at the very least, that he has been living within his partner, invading her space, virtually telling her, "Since I live within you I know what you are."

The Exception

He comes to this full realization, but then falls under the influence of family or culture—believing "real men" are in charge of women—and denies it all. He blocks his realizations from his mind and he becomes angry and hostile, so that he can feel strong enough to fend off his insights and stay in the dark with his dream woman.

HE DOESN'T WANT TO HARM HIS CHILDREN

This man is conscious enough to realize that by being defined, oppressed, and abused in his childhood, he lost touch with himself. It is clear to him that if he attempts to define his own children or to verbally abuse their mother, they will become as disconnected and controlling as he is. One man who indulged in verbal abuse said, "Much of my personal mission in life has been to strive not to pass these kinds of sorrows on to my children. I am so motivated to change now that I have more enlightenment."

The Exception

He forgets that his children are separate people and uses them as pawns to fight his partner. He is so disconnected that he attempts to brainwash them into bonding with him against their mother.

HE DOESN'T WANT TO BE LIKE HIS FATHER

A verbally abusive man who remembers his resentment when his father defined him may be motivated to change. One man who did not want to be like his father, said of his partner, "What she shared with me about what I did sounded almost exactly like what my father did to me. I'm awestruck that I did exactly what I resented so much in that man. My hope is that I am not like my father."

The Exception

He convinces himself that his partner doesn't see him like he sees his father, and he does not want to, or cannot, do the work required to access the qualities and functions he never developed in order to dispel his dream woman.

HE DOESN'T WANT TO BE SEEN ACTING AS IF HE IS HIS PARTNER

Once the verbally abusive man realizes that he has been defining his partner's inner experience—in effect, her reality—he is often motivated to stop. He doesn't want to be locked into pretending to know what his partner is, thinks, feels, etc., as if he were she—as if he were a woman.

The verbally abusive man is most motivated to change when he realizes that by telling his partner, "You're too sensitive," or, "You're trying to start a fight," he is, in effect, telling her, "I live within you. I know what you feel. I know that it is not how you're supposed to feel." He again shows himself to be within his partner, and he wants to stop.

The Exception

He believes that his word is like the word of God, that if he says she is too sensitive or that she doesn't have a sense of humor, it is a fact. He is quite proud of his dominance over her, even telling others about it. He either has no conscience or has a psychopathic personality.

HE WANTS TO BE THE PERSON HE ALWAYS THOUGHT HE WAS

When he wakes up to his behavior, he is shocked at the disparity between the way he sees himself and the way he actually behaves. His image to the world doesn't match his behavior behind closed doors. When he sees the Agreement, he sees himself as his partner sees him. Usually, this is the first time he even has a glimmer of the truth about himself.

The Exception

He flushes the Agreement down the toilet. Or he says, "These examples are all what *you* say, so I don't have to agree to anything." He always saw himself as right no matter what, so his image is not damaged. He is so completely merged with his partner, he finds it difficult to actually tell the difference between what he says and what she says.

HE DOESN'T WANT TO LIE

He realizes that when he defines his partner, he is intent on deceiving her in order to silence or diminish her. He realizes that he is lying to her. Either by religious training or in some other way, it has been instilled in him that lying is the worst thing he can do.

The Exception

He is either deeply confused because his confabulations seem so much like memory to him that he believes them despite evidence to the contrary, or he does not think that a lie to his partner should matter at all because he sees her as having wronged him by acting separately. Her separateness, her personhood, is what gives him a sense of being attacked and creates the confabulations that explain it.

HE DOESN'T WANT HIS PARTNER TO FEAR HIS "CRAZINESS"

Most verbally abusive men are shocked to know that their partners fear them—shocked to know that their partners fear their irrationality, their tempers, their impenetrable staring silences, and the constant pain of being defined. They are stunned to know that their partners are wondering if they are living with crazy men whom only they can see, or if they are losing their minds. They've never thought that when they deny what they've just said, their partners worry that they are with, or married to, or even dependent on, a multiple personality—a person who has no knowledge of what he just said, as in "I never said that. We never had that conversation. I don't know what you're talking about." This is terrifying. The partner who hears this may never feel that she can trust him again.

The Exception

People who are so disconnected from themselves that they do not even perceive their common humanity have no conscience. They cannot feel contrite and may be psychopathic. A psychopath would not feel concern, trepidation, guilt, or remorse if he realized that his partner was afraid of him. On the contrary, he may feel so able to control her that her fear would be reassuring to him. "She won't go against me now. She'd be afraid to leave." And all the while, his unconscious, in accord with his knowledge of her fear, would, if it could speak, say, "This body won't leave me now; it's a safe harbor for the dream woman."

HE IS BASICALLY A GOOD MAN WHO HAS THE COURAGE TO CHANGE

A man, whom I'll call Tom, very kindly gave me permission to quote a letter he wrote to his friends in a men's group. His courage is sorely needed in the world today, and I am confident that, because it is so strong and real, it will take him far and most amazingly affect a great many people. What is to some men something to be denied or hidden away—knowledge of some men's defining and control of women—is now a beacon to light the path of change. With knowledge and determination they may have the courage to follow the path of change so that we can all have a better world.

Tom wrote:

> "I'm currently reading *The Verbally Abusive Relationship*. It was very hard to read at first because it so much talked about me. It spelled out my relationship with anger quite well—in fact, too well. The more I read, the more I have come to realize how badly my anger and control issues have affected how my bride looks at me and how my two boys act around me. Why they sometimes flinch when I reach up to give them a hug or pat on the back for doing something good. I've been married now for 15+ years and have been angry for most of those years. Bosses, co-workers, friends, and family rarely ever see my abusive ways. My spouse and kids get it daily or weekly depending on how 'my week' is going at work or play.

"Reading about 'me' in this book is chilling. Or to be exact, men just like me. I have identified with many of the scenarios. It makes me sad to know that I too am one of those men who are weak and look to control others by acting out and controlling them by words and actions.

"Our families deserve better, and we as leaders in our church and as men's group leaders need to step up and be an example of this. After all, who will do this for all men if not the leaders? And how can we call ourselves Spiritual Heads of our Households if we exact this price on our families? What message does this send to our sons and daughters on how their relationships, problems, and anxieties should be handled?"

Men like Tom are likely to change if they commit to doing the work required. There is no basic exception that would prevent these men from being able to change.

HE IS BOTH ACCOUNTABLE AND REPENTANT

He is distressed and saddened, not so much for himself—that he might lose his partner—but rather, that he has caused her so much emotional pain and mental anguish. He wants to right the wrongs he has perpetrated on her and deeply regrets that he has defined her. He feels accountable. With accountability, he feels guilt that he silenced her or vented his anger on her, completely heedless of the impact of his behavior. He acknowledges and deeply regrets his behavior and is mature enough to turn his regret into determination to change. He is fully committed to doing the work to change.

This man is most likely to change and there is no general exception to his being able to change, if he does not give up on himself and his commitment to change.

HE THINKS HE IS JUSTIFIED

Looking back over the last thousand women or so that I have talked to, or even the accounts of the thousands of women registered on the VerbalAbuse.com bulletin board, there is one universal experience in particular that no one has ever refuted. It is that the verbally abusive man either denies that he is verbally abusing his partner when he is doing just that, or he tells her in some way that she made him do it.

Both the verbally abusive man's denial and blame state that he is not responsible for his behavior.

How can the partner motivate the verbally abusive man to change, if he hasn't even acknowledged that there is something in his behavior that requires change? After all, as I've said in previous chapters, he often truly believes anything he says is nothing compared to what his partner does to him. No one can change their behavior if they don't see how they are behaving and that nothing justifies that behavior.

After years of trying to get the verbally abusive man to see what he is doing, his partner will have a new tool, the Agreement. It gives the verbally abusive man what is often his first clue that he has been pretending to be his partner, to be living in her, knowing what she is supposed to do, say, think, etc. In a way, it will jump-start the process of change, if it is at all possible for him to change, because he will see what he says in the Agreement. He will see that his statements are irrational. He will also see that the only way he could tell his partner what she is and what she feels, etc., is if he did, in fact pretend to *be* her.

Some part of him may waken, and if his unconscious could speak it might say, "I pretend to be you, a woman, because I am afraid of staying in my own body/mind. I must invade your very soul to tell you your motives. I must live within you in order to feel whole because I have lost so much of myself. I must control you to keep you near. And my fear of standing on my own two feet is seen as cowardice by the world, but now the world has seen me. There is nothing to do but change or continue in pursuit of the unattainable: the rest of myself. I cannot own it, but maybe I can integrate it." Thus, he may realize that *change is essential.*

8

HOW TO PREPARE FOR THE AGREEMENT

WHAT WILL BE HAPPENING IN your relationship before you present the Agreement to your mate? Generally speaking, you will be making a transition from how your relationship was, to, hopefully, what it might be. Even before you write and present the Agreement to him, you might begin the process of waking up your mate to the reality of his behavior.

The general goal is that you show him in some way that you hear what he is saying, that he is responsible for saying it, and that it is incomprehensible. Using these strategies, you needn't defend yourself.

For example, rather than explaining to him just how you feel and why when he says or does something that hurts or disturbs you, you can begin responding to him in a way that calls attention to his behavior. If in the past, you explained to him what was bothering you, he obviously chose not to hear you, or you wouldn't be in need of the Agreement. He ignored you, not only because he judged himself right and you wrong, but also, as we've seen, he feels attacked just hearing your "real voice" where his dream woman is supposed to be. Feeling attacked, he will want to get back at you. His unconscious may be screaming, "I'm being severed from reality! Where is the rest of me? Where is my dream woman? How could you do this to me? How could you show up where my dream woman should be?"

Realizing that verbal abuse is not rational, it becomes clear that the man indulging in it can't hear a rational response from his partner. But it is difficult for the partner not to respond with a rational explanation. For instance, she may say she didn't deserve to be yelled at, or she didn't do what she is being accused of, even when she knows that rational explanations just won't work. It takes enormous conscious effort for the partner not to explain herself to her mate. It usually seems to her that he is rational and will apologize and not do it again.

Women often talk about how hard it is to remember that there is no point in their ever responding rationally to verbal abuse, even when they know that verbal abuse is a lie. However, it is important for you to keep in mind that since the verbal abuse is a lie, it is incomprehensible. You must decide to see it as so untrue, so unimaginable, so unreal, that you simply say, "What?" or "What did you say?" or "What are you doing?" This may gently prod him toward hearing himself if he starts defining you in any way (see Appendix A, page 227, for lists of defining statements).

If in the past you told him, "Stop!" when he was abusive and he didn't, it is likely that he accused *you* of being abusive, saying, "Now you're giving me orders and trying to control me. That's abuse!"

A good response to this lie is to simply say, "What?" or even, "Did I just hear you tell me what I was trying to do? What did you say?" After all, he just told you what your motives were and what you were trying to do, as if he were you.

Please note that when the verbally abusive man hears "Stop!" or "Stop it!" and tells you that you are trying to control him—if he does seem to believe this—it could be helpful to have a friend, counselor, minister, rabbi, or other person he respects explain to him that "stop" is a protection against assault or invasion.

Consider this example: Two tribes in ancient times are in a forest and one tribe starts shooting arrows at the other. The other tribe puts up bales of hay to keep the arrows from piercing them. The word "stop" is like a bale of hay: It is an attempt to stop the slings and arrows of verbal abuse from penetrating the partner's psyche.

Ultimately, since you know that blaming is a category of verbal abuse, it should be easier not to blame yourself in any way for his behavior. You can see it as abusive no matter how much he blames you, tells you that you "made" him mad, or tells you that it is your fault.

THE BEST DEFENSE IS NO DEFENSE

In order to begin the process of change, the verbally abusive man has to recognize what he is doing when he is doing it. Naturally, you, as his partner, have the most opportunity to wake him up the moment he defines you. If you have tried before, and he only became angrier and more abusive, you can try the following strategies, unless he has shown some sign of being dangerous, or your intuition warns you off.

In the case where there is no danger and you have just heard your husband yelling that, for instance, you should know where something is that he misplaced, if you say, "I feel bad when you yell at me like that," he will probably reply, "You're too sensitive."

Since telling the verbally abusive man how you feel or explaining why he shouldn't yell doesn't work, let's review a few of the more effective responses. I present them in ascending order from gentle to outraged. The minute you hear the abuse, I suggest you use any of the following:

> *"What?"*
> *"What did you say?"*
> *"What are you doing?"*
> *"Would you please repeat that while I write it down?"*
> *"Would you repeat that, please, so I can tape it and not forget it?"*
> *"It sounds like you're telling me [whatever he's saying]."*

A few men to whom I have given consultations have pointed out that in their communities, if a person said "What?" to someone, it was a signal for a serious fight. For most people, "what" means "pardon"—it means they were distracted, or didn't catch what was said for some reason. If the man you are responding to comes from the culture that hears "What?" as a challenge to fight, then it is best to say, "What *did you say?*" If the kind of abuse that you experience is withholding, he might walk away when you are talking. In this case, saying, "What are you doing?" will work just fine. If you try any of the previous phrases, and he continues to define you, try saying the following:

> *"You're not me. Please don't tell me [whatever he's saying]."*
> *"Please stop pretending to be me."*
> *"Please stop pretending to live within me and know what I am."*
> *"Please stop pretending to be me and know what I am."*
> *"Please stop pretending to be a woman."*
> *"You're not me. Please get out."*

If he insists on defining you—staying within you, so to speak—I suggest a final resort: Hold up your hand, palm out, arm straight, like one does to show "stop," while lowering your voice to a very deep resonance, then command him out, with "Get out now." These words should be spoken three times, very slowly and with authority, like an exorcism, while your body is centered and your knees are slightly bent so you appear sturdy and strong. This works very well for some women; if it doesn't work for you, holding up a cross or other meaningful symbol might.

Generally, if the previous strategies don't work, the following ones might be helpful. After you hear him define you twice, say, "That's what I thought you said," and then take out a little notebook from your pocket or nearby, just for such occasions. Say, "Hold on, please. I need to write that down!" then write down the date, glance at a watch or a clock (or ask him for the time), and then write down the time and what he said. This will give you useful sentences for the Agreement coming up in Chapter 10. And he will know that there is a record of what he is saying to you. Is he proud of what he says? Is he ashamed? Is he confused? Does he fear that the outside world will know about his inside world? Only he knows, but it is the beginning of a wakeup call.

Alternatively, you can carry a small, voice-activated, digital recorder because you can store many hours on it. When he indulges in verbal abuse, you can hold it up while saying, "What did you say?" Of course, if he has been physically violent or threatened violence, instead of stopping what he is saying, he may become violent because he does not want anyone to hear what he is doing. It is all-important that you trust your experience and your intuition, and you must judge this for yourself. At all times you must be fiercely protective of yourself.

Even if he is too scary to confront with any comment, you should not defend yourself. As I noted earlier, explanations just make him the judge and the jury. Additionally, when you explain yourself, wanting him to agree that what he said was not okay, he sees that as deferring to him, as if you were wholly dependent on him.

Until he sees the Agreement, he doesn't know what he doesn't know: that he has, for the most part, seemed to think he was you. Obviously, as long as he is under that illusion, he will tell you what you are, what you think, what you should do, what you feel, what you want, what you need, etc., as if he lived within you and knew.

If the verbally abusive man wakes up to what he is doing, wants a healthy relationship, and does the work to change, he may have such a relationship either in the future with someone else or with you—but only if you still want a relationship with him. Let's briefly look again at what constitutes a relationship: Scientifically, it is an interchange between two beings (or living systems) open to the exchange of information between them. Information can even be the molecules exchanged between the plant and its environment. They exchange or relate to each other.

Clearly, when one person defines the other, the person doing the defining (abusing), has closed off from the real person. When a person is told what they are, think, feel, and so forth, it is not only a lie told to them about themselves, but also it means that the abuser is closed off from the real person. The abuser cannot really hear, see, and take in information from the real person. It is as if he sees someone else. For instance, if the abuser says, "You're too sensitive" or "You're not listening," he is talking to someone whom he defines as "made wrong" or as "not listening." So, the real person isn't seen or heard. It is as if a wall has arisen between the verbally abusive man and his partner. This is why, when a man defines his partner, she feels pain. At some level, she experiences the end of the relationship.

WHAT IS NORMAL CONVERSATION?

While you are encouraging change, it can be helpful for you to review what is normal conversation in a relationship. Even if you come from a highly conscious and functional home, hearing yourself defined over time can desensitize you to the abuse. In fact, most partners do become desensitized, forgetful of what just shocked and confused them because verbal abuse assaults their minds.

Here are some examples of abusive versus healthy dialogue.

Abusive: You can't take a joke.
Healthy: What bothered you about that joke?

Abusive: You're trying to start a fight.
Healthy: What do you want to talk about?

Abusive: You're jumping to conclusions.
Healthy: How did you come to that conclusion?

Abusive: You're too sensitive.
Healthy: Please tell me what's upset you.

Abusive: You're so lazy.
Healthy: Are you behind schedule? Do you need some help?

Abusive: You can't do anything right.
Healthy: What happened? Can I help? Want to talk about it?

Abusive: You're blowing it out of proportion.
Healthy: How do you feel? What is it like for you?

Abusive: You're a real nag.
Healthy: I'm sorry I didn't do what I said I'd do.

Abusive: You think you know it all.

Healthy: What do you have in mind? What do you think about this?

As the partner of a verbally abusive man, you might not have heard normal conversations as described above in many years. And your mate has not heard your complaints and requests. How can you be heard? If there is any possibility of your being heard, I believe it is most likely if you present the information you are giving your mate in a kind of multimedia way. From that standpoint, presenting the Agreement with impact is very important. I will show you how in the next chapter. After all, what is the value of the Agreement if it is only given a cursory glance by the verbally abusive man?

9

HOW TO PRESENT
THE AGREEMENT

IN MANY CASES, THE PARTNER of a verbally abusive man has
spent five, ten, or more years trying to be understood and trying to understand what is wrong in the relationship. For instance,
she thinks her mate cannot understand her because she hasn't
expressed herself correctly, or she can't get his attention because
she doesn't have anything really interesting to say since she isn't
up on the latest news. But actually, to really be seen, heard, and
understood, she would have to make a strong impact on her mate.
Consequently, the way the Agreement is presented is almost as
important as what is in it—at least as far as her mate's hearing her
is concerned. It will need to be presented with the most impact
possible.

Even before presenting the Agreement, it's helpful for you to have a good understanding of how your mate's illusionary Dream Woman, his undeveloped unlived self, impacts the relationship. The more information you have, the more effective you will be in taking the necessary steps to prepare, write, present, and follow up with the Agreement. Additionally, by understanding what is wrong with your abuser, you will be less inclined to defend yourself and more able to respond effectively to any verbal abuse, in the way it describes.

The Agreement often gives the verbally abusive man his first inkling that something is seriously wrong in his relationship, and it can even give him a glimmer of what it is. Since he generally can't hear his partner without losing his unlived self, when she presents it to him, what he does hear will likely come as a shock, chiefly because he will believe that he never heard anything like it before. Often a man will call for help when his partner has left or filed for divorce, saying he was shocked that she saw him as verbally abusive. No matter how many times these men were asked not to talk "like that," they never thought of themselves as abusive, nor did they think they should try to address their partners in a different way, or even inquire as to what bothered them.

If you divorce him before he sees his own behavior in the Agreement, he may end up as many men have, saying he was blindsided; he therefore may be much more difficult to deal with. Not that you didn't tell him his behavior was unacceptable. You did, of course, but he couldn't hear you. And some verbally abusive men will be difficult under any circumstances. Their goal in life is to win at all costs, right or wrong. Some men typically have three or four relationships or marriages in which their partners leave before they are willing to hear their current partner and look at their own behavior. Then, if they aren't psychopathic and don't have a personality disorder, they may try to change.

If you have already left the relationship, you may still present your mate with an Agreement that has been modified to be a statement of why you left. If you will never see him again, you may not care to present it, but if there are children involved and you will see him again, it may be worthwhile at least to e-mail it to him as a statement. If he sees why you left, he may be less inclined to blame you for everything and to take his anger out on you by creating a huge custody battle, or defaming you to the children.

If you haven't left the relationship and you present the Agreement to your mate, he may realize that you are serious and that you might leave. The more concerned he is that you might leave, the more he will try to get you to stay—that is, unless he has found another body for his dream woman.

In his attempts to keep you, he may alternately offer you gifts if you will stay and threaten you with dire consequences if you leave. At this early stage, it might not occur to the verbally abusive man to address you as a real person—to simply ask you what you require of him in the way of change. Nor does it occur to him that a reward/punishment system might work with a puppy but not necessarily on you. Many women who receive threats upon leaving their abusers remark that threats only remind them of why they left in the first place. Some threats partners have told me about include those listed below:

"I'll break you."
"I'll take the kids."
"I'll make sure no one will hire you."
"You'll be a bag lady."
"I'll make your life a living hell."
"I'll kill you."
"I'll kill myself."

Take any threat seriously and report it to your lawyer or to the police, depending on whether it is a legal or life-and-death matter. You may be able to get a restraining order or an order of protection if you are threatened with harm. Always remember that a man who threatens can be very dangerous. A threat against your life or a threat of injury is the assault part of "assault and battery."

It is important to keep in mind that the goal of the Agreement, beyond waking up the verbally abusive man, is that you, as a couple, will bond together against the problem. You and your mate are not against *each other*. When you both sign the Agreement, you are, in effect, agreeing to be bonded together against verbal abuse. It helps to see verbal abuse as a dark cloud that settles on your relationship. The verbal abuser doesn't see it when he is immersed in it, but you can and so, too, can any witnesses.

PREAGREEMENT STEPS

Not knowing whether your mate will improve or become so detached from himself and the real issues that he becomes violent, I recommend that you try to take the following specific steps before writing up your Agreement.

1. Integrate as much information about verbal abuse as you can.

Review the previous chapters and read other books on verbal abuse so the preliminary information is well integrated in your psyche. This will make it much easier for you to present the Agreement and to respond to any violations. You benefit if you have done everything you can to gain clarity about your situation, and know that you have the means to stop or leave the emotional pain and mental anguish verbal abuse creates.

2. Get support.

Your best strategy for support is to tell what you are doing, and why, to all *supportive and trustworthy* relatives, friends, counselors, professionals, and members of any religious community to which you belong. Then, if your mate becomes vicious or violent, you'll have the support you need. Although the Agreement will be drafted in a nonaccusatory style, one never knows how anyone will react to it.

3. Make a list.

To write the Agreement, you will need to have a list of as many verbally abusive statements as you can recall. These are the things you have heard from your mate in his attempts to define you. Appendix A, page 227, lists common defining statements, some of which you might have heard from him. Look over the lists with this question in mind: "Has he said this to me?" You will then be able to make a comprehensive list of the abusive comments that you have heard from your mate. You will be using these statements as examples in your Agreement, so include all that you've heard, as well as other similar ones that might not be in the appendix.

4. Find a time and a place to prepare.

If you don't have a computer, you will need to plan where and when you will type up and print two copies of the Agreement. It is fairly simple and best done on a computer so you can print it for the presentation and e-mail it to your mate, if he has e-mail, so that he may add to it. If you don't have access to your own computer, I recommend that you write the Agreement, then type and print two copies at a full-service copy center where you can use the computer for a nominal fee and can make a digital copy for future reference. One printed copy is for you to keep, and one you will give to your abuser, but only after you have read the Agreement to him.

Basically, you're going to write up the Agreement and present it to your verbally abusive man. You will agree to sign the Agreement after you review any input from him. In other words, you're going to sign the Agreement even if you didn't indulge in verbally abusive behavior. You must never, however, sign anything you don't agree to; if there is anything you or your mate cannot agree to, you both cross it out.

5. Plan your presentation.

Before presenting the Agreement, it is important to plan the best place and time to present it. It may be your own living room, it may be at a counselor's, or anyplace you feel safe. Here are some suggestions to think about when planning your presentation:

a. Plan to present it in front of a witness, at the office of a therapist, counselor, minister, or rabbi where the witness would know ahead of time what you planned and that witnessing is all you want from this person.

b. Plan to present it in a quiet but public spot such as at a picnic bench in the park or a secluded and quiet corner in a large hotel lobby.

c. Plan to present it at home with a friend or relative present.

d. If you feel safe presenting the Agreement in private, then do so.

Though the Agreement is only a first step, it is the step that has a possibility of waking him up to the fact that he defines you and that he has pretended to be you or in your body/mind/soul for a long time. He may also begin to realize that he cannot define your inner world and be rational at the same time. And even if it does not wake him up, it now becomes a ground rule about his communications. If either of you breaks the Agreement, you will signal the other and follow the Agreement to correct the problem—that is, to get verbal abuse out of your relationship.

The verbally abusive man is not inclined to hear what his partner says and has an enormous resistance to doing what she asks him to do when it doesn't fit with what his dream woman would ask. Consequently, it will be well worth a few hours of time and energy to make the presentation of the Agreement as clear and impactful as possible.

Some women ask if presenting the Agreement might not accelerate the verbal abuse to such an extent that their mate would become physically violent. I tell them that if they have been physically assaulted, hit, pushed, shoved, or have faced frightening rages, then it would be better to present the Agreement in a therapist's or counselor's office, or in a public but quiet place. If you feel any fear or if he has threatened you or has hurt you physically, it is better to very carefully plan to leave, and to get assistance from a domestic violence prevention organization.

If he has not been violent, however, he is less likely to accelerate his abuse once he understands that he will be invited to add to the Agreement. He will be a participant and, since the Agreement states that both parties agree that neither will do "whatever," it is clearly binding to both parties. You will invite him to write in, or to e-mail back in a different font or color, what he wants to add to the Agreement. For all these reasons, he is more likely going to feel that it is a mutual agreement. Finally, you'll explain to him in the beginning that this Agreement is designed to make your relationship happier.

6. Set up the meeting with safety first.

When you have written the Agreement as laid out in the next chapter and you are ready to present it to him, make an appointment with him at your prearranged place. Once you have decided on the best location to meet with him, set up the appointment by telling him that you want to meet with him because you have something very important to discuss with him. Suggest a couple of times that don't conflict with your schedule or with his and ask him if one would work for him. He may want to know what it is you want to talk about. It is best to tell him, "I'd love to go over it with you at the meeting. For now, I want you to know I have some basic ideas about how to make our relationship better."

Above all, please consider whether it is safe to present the Agreement to him. If his abuse is overt, if he flies into rages, if he has been violent, demonstrated violence, or threatened violence, then it's imperative that you present the Agreement in as safe a place as possible.

PRESENTATION OF THE AGREEMENT

Because of the way you present the Agreement, your mate is likely to hear you. It may be the first time in a long time that he actually does. Part of its impact is due to the formal style the Agreement is written in, and part of its impact is from the formal way you will present it to him.

To present the Agreement effectively, it is important that you have two tape or digital recorders. Set one on the table at the meeting and one on a side table or the floor. You can leave this second one on until the meeting is over so you will have a record of the entire exchange. This will ensure that both you and your mate will each have an audio record of the Agreement. (You keep the extended-play version.)

After you have prepared the Agreement (Chapter 10) and made two copies, one for yourself and one for him, you will read it to him at the planned meeting. Under no circumstances are you to give him his paper copy until you have read it to him. If you hand him his copy before reading it aloud to him, it is likely that he will start writing on it and not listen to you.

When you meet him, before you start, turn on the tape recorders. Then tell him that you have something to read to him. Tell him that when you finish reading it, you will give him his copy so that he can add whatever he wants to it, as well as a tape recording of it. When you finish reading it to him, stop the tape in front of you and hand it to him along with his copy of the Agreement. You could say something like, "Here's the hard copy and here's a tape. I will also e-mail you a copy so that you can make any additions you want." Ask him to please add any additions or changes in a different font or color since it is a mutual agreement. And ask him to get back to you with it in a few days, or whatever you deem best based on your schedules, but not more than a week. Set up a firm time to meet again to initial or sign the Agreement.

If he starts talking about the Agreement before your next meeting, attempting to put it down or to argue points in it, say that you look forward to seeing his contribution to the Agreement at your next meeting and that you will discuss his questions then. It is okay to remind him that you look forward to seeing his additions to the Agreement in a different font or color, unless he pencils them in. If you hear him defining you, say "What?" or "What did you say?" and if he walks away when you are talking with him, ask, "What are you doing?"

Signing the Agreement

When you meet for the second time at the agreed-upon time, read over any changes he has made or text he as added to the Agreement, suggest that you each cross off anything you cannot agree to, and sign it.

It is important to realize that signing the Agreement doesn't make the verbally abusive man change. Rather, if he agrees that neither party will define the other, according to the Agreement, then you will have achieved a first step in waking him up. *It may be the first time that he actually sees and hears what you say to him.* Most important, the Agreement will state that neither person lives within the other and knows what he or she is, thinks, feels, etc. (This sentence should be in bold large letters—in red, if you have a color printer.) *This may be the first time that the verbally abusive man realizes that he has pretended to be his partner, to know what she is, thinks, feels, etc.* If he doesn't get this at first, the idea may begin to filter into his psyche.

If the Agreement Is Broken

The Agreement also spells out what to say if either party hears themselves defined. If you, for instance, give the signal "What?" when you hear yourself defined, your mate has agreed to take the signal as a clear indicator that he has said something that may be abusive. He must rerun the statement through his mind and ask himself, "Am I in any way defining my partner, or lying to her?" He then rephrases the comment as he has agreed. Likewise, if you hear the signal, you too must check your thoughts, recall what you said, and if it is abusive, rephrase it.

This signal is built into the Agreement because in everyday conversation one person may define another without thinking, such as by saying, "You shouldn't wear that." The "I take it back" sentence would be something like, "Sorry, I can't tell you what to wear."

THE AGREEMENT IS EFFECTIVE

The Agreement is effective because it uses examples that are the exact verbally abusive statements that you have heard from your mate. When he sees, hears, and reads such familiar sentences, he may recognize them as his own. On the other hand, he probably wouldn't recognize them if you just told him about them and they weren't in the Agreement. The Agreement is a very compelling way to bring awareness, and I know of no more certain way for you to be heard than by presenting the Agreement in the way I've described.

- It may be the first time he receives an Agreement in four ways: read to him, printed on a hard copy, on an audio-tape, and in his e-mail.
- It may be the first time he realizes that he has been, at some level, living within you, not accepting your separateness.
- It may be the first time he realizes that he has acted irrationally on many occasions.
- It may be the first time he actually hears you as if you were, in fact, a separate person.
- It may be the first time he takes you seriously.
- It may be the first time he realizes that his relationship may be in jeopardy.

THE AGREEMENT IS MUTUAL

Before turning to the sample Agreement in the next chapter, let's review the nature of the Agreement. Primarily, it is mutual. Even though you may rarely or never verbally abuse your mate, hit him, threaten him, or respond to abuse with similar abuse, for the Agreement to work, it must be designed in such a way that both you and he agree to it. In other words, it won't say, "You may not . . ." It will instead say, "Neither person will . . ."

Since the verbally abusive man frequently feels attacked, he often describes his life as a battle with his partner, or like being at war against her. He cannot comprehend an Agreement that tells him that he may not do certain things. To him the war is, at the very least, half his partner's fault. From his perspective, a nonmutual Agreement would be like telling him to lay down his weapons while he is at war, which to him is crazy.

Even though you might like him to promise not to do many things, he will be much more inclined to agree to stop defining you if he knows that you agree not to define him back. If, on the other hand, you do define him—say, you call him a name every time he calls you one or put him down when he gives you orders—this does not affect the Agreement in any negative way. You simply put in your comments along with his in the examples sections. Consequently, your mate will know that it is mutual.

If the Agreement isn't mutual, in terms of both persons agreeing not to say certain things, the verbally abusive man could spend a great deal of time trying to convince you that you define him as much as or more than he defines you. In fact, given the opportunity, people who indulge in verbal abuse in relationships are willing to debate the issue for any number of possible life-times with their partners. By diverting from the problem with accusations—such as, "You do this way more than I do," "You verbally abuse me at least 80 percent of the time," or "This is totally a fifty-fifty thing"—he can avoid even hearing that you want him to change. He might keep you sidetracked defending yourself against the accusations indefinitely. Additionally, even if you haven't defined him, or only occasionally called him a name because you couldn't make him stop verbally abusing you, it is simply safer to include yourself in the Agreement.

One very passively aggressive man diverted his partner for years by saying, "I don't want to argue," if she said something like, "Do you want to go to Disneyland this summer?"

He would say, "I don't want to argue about it."

Then she would say, "Do you have any comment about the idea of going to Disneyland?"

He would say, "I just don't want to argue with you."

She would then say, "I'd like to hear your comment on my idea. It's just an idea. I'm not trying to argue."

Then he'd say, "I told you, I don't want to argue with you."

Then she'd say, "I'm not arguing."

He'd say, "You are. I told you I don't want to argue," and he would walk away.

To stop any diversions, the partner must repeat the question: "Do you want to go to Disneyland this summer?" until he answers the question.

The Agreement will state that both parties agree to repeat the question until the other responds. "Yes," "No," "I don't know," or "I'll get back to you on that," are all acceptable responses.

Another important reason to write the Agreement as mutual and something both of you agree to is that from the moment it is signed, your mutual goal with your cosigner is that verbal abuse will end. A debate over who verbally abused whom, what percent of the time, is just a diversion from that goal. By agreeing that you will not tell him, for instance, what he is (even if you haven't ever defined him), and his agreeing that he won't define you, you are bonded together in the goal of stopping verbal abuse. What matters is that verbal abuse not occur any more in the relationship. Women often fear that no one will believe them when they say they don't deserve to be put down or in any way verbally abused, and they don't indulge in verbal abuse. As one woman wrote to me, "I fear that he is going to try to convince you that this is at least fifty percent my fault (like he has done to four counselors) instead of focusing on himself."

I assured this woman that what percent of fault was ascribed to which partner may have made some difference to the counselors, but it surely does not have anything to do with whether verbal abuse shows up in the relationship, from this moment forward. The debate is simply a diversion from the problem.

If you haven't made the Agreement mutual and later on, in frustration over his breaking the Agreement, you forget yourself and in some way define him, he could claim that the Agreement is over. He might say everything is your fault and that *you* are verbally abusing *him*. And he may also say that whatever he says is justified because you're the abuser! But if the Agreement is mutual and he hears himself defined, he may be willing to respond as stated in the Agreement. You will have likewise agreed to respond in a specific way if you hear yourself defined. The goal is that you and your mate are bonded together against the problem of verbal abuse and both are subject to the Agreement.

The Agreement is mutual, not only because both parties agree to its terms, but also because both have an opportunity to contribute to it. If your verbally abusive man adds examples of statements that you have never said to him, go ahead and sign it anyway. You would only be agreeing (along with him) not to say something you've never said. This is not likely to become a problem.

This highly motivating Agreement will be essential to waking the abuser. The next chapter explains how to draft an Agreement that is designed to wake the abuser so that he not only sees, word for word, what he says, but also has the opportunity to realize how irrational his behavior has been. He may see that he has pretended *to be* you. The next chapter also shows a sample Agreement.

Even if you are not in an abusive relationship but are assisting someone who is, it may be very helpful for you to read the Agreement. Please note that this Agreement could be used in any relationship, and if a man is experiencing verbal abuse from his partner, he too can initiate it.

10

HOW TO WRITE THE AGREEMENT

THIS CHAPTER IS WRITTEN SPECIFICALLY for the partner of a verbal abuser. If, however, you are not in a verbally abusive relationship but want to know more about how verbal abuse in any situation defines you, I believe that it will give you insights and tools to use the rest of your life. It will also give you the kind of information you can use to support anyone, be it friend, relative, or acquaintance, whom you know to be in a verbally abusive relationship. Of course, it is also a tool for therapists who work with sufferers of verbal abuse, as well as for those who perpetrate verbal abuse but want to change.

If you suspect that you, yourself, are verbally abusive to anyone, then the Agreement will also be helpful in allowing you to see what you are doing and it will, hopefully, motivate you to do the recommended work that I describe in later chapters.

If you are planning on presenting the Agreement, most likely you will be writing it up and presenting it to the man who has verbally abused you. This is a one-time opportunity to put all the verbal abuse in a special format that says, in effect, "These are examples of one person telling the other what they are, what they think, what they are trying to do, and so forth—and, we both agree not to do that."

In order to make the most of the Agreement, I highly recommend you use as many examples as you can—every verbally abusive statement you have ever heard from the verbally abusive man in your life. The more examples you have, the more likely the abuser will notice that he has been doing something strange, that is, defining his partner's inner world, inner experience, inner feelings, and so forth as if he were her. Or, he may simply define her as nonexistent by finding ways to avoid responding to her.

THE FIVE PARTS OF THE AGREEMENT

The Agreement has five parts. Part I states what both the partner and the verbally abusive man agree they will not to say to each other. It is about verbal abuse. Part II states why neither person will define the other. Part III states what both parties agree not to do. Part IV states what both parties agree to do. Part V states how both parties agree to respond if the Agreement is broken.

I recommend that you do *not* consult with your mate about verbal abuse. Do not mention verbal abuse to him. After you present the Agreement to him, he will have time to add anything he wants to it. Typically, when a verbally abusive man hears the words "verbal abuse," his immediate response is, "That's what you do." If he sees my book *The Verbally Abusive Relationship*, he typically says, "That's what you do," or he tears it up, or throws it away. Some men do take the information to heart and see what they've done, but that is not something you can count on. If you are leaving him, or have just left him, then you will see on page 135 how to turn the Agreement into a statement of why you have done so.

Following are instructions on how to develop each part.

Part I

Part I is about what you both agree not to say. To begin, please make a list of sentences you have heard that you would call verbally abusive. If you have read *The Verbally Abusive Relationship*, you may have noticed that I broke verbal abuse into categories such as discounting, ordering, or blaming. You will not be breaking the verbally abusive statements into these categories for the Agreement. Instead, the Agreement will organize the verbally abusive statements according to what they tell you—that is, according to how they define you. To organize them this way, every time you recall an abusive statement, simply ask yourself, "What is this telling me? Is it telling me what I *think*? Is it telling me what I *am*? Is it telling me what I'm *doing*?" and so forth. For example, your mate might say, "You're too sensitive," which tells you what you *are*. Then put that statement on your list under "what he says you are."

Appendix A, page 227, contains a comprehensive breakout of verbally abusive statements. I suggest that if you have experienced verbal abuse in any situation, you go over all the lists to see if any of the verbally abusive statements are ones you've heard. If they are, and you are writing up an Agreement, please be sure to put them on your list. If they remind you of other statements, then use the ones you have heard. Only the statements that you have heard the verbally abusive man speak will resonate in his memory.

Of special note is the very covert verbal abuser who defines by implication and insinuation, or gives his partner the silent treatment, or walks away when she is talking. Since he is so covert, he may have difficulty realizing that he is abusive at all. It is as if his denial of what he is doing shows up in the abuse itself. The covert abuser turns the defining statements into questions or accusations. Consequently, the Agreement can include an additional section that states that both parties agree that neither will define the other by implication or insinuation. See Appendix A, List 4, page 244.

Here's an example. A woman who is raising a large family and managing it all with grace and kindness, but is becoming exhausted and ill from a seemingly never-ending assault by her husband, said to me, "My husband doesn't tell me, 'You don't think,' or 'You're stupid,' but a day doesn't go by that he doesn't imply that I've done something thoughtless, wrong, or without intelligence."

She continued, "He yells things like, 'What *were* you thinking?' all the time. He shouts this whenever something doesn't match his idea of what should be happening. He is very clever about it. He doesn't use 'you' statements like, 'You don't do your share,' but instead says such things as, 'When will you do your part in this marriage?'"

Part II

Part II is about *why* both parties agree not to say defining (verbally abusive) comments to each other. Even if you haven't defined your mate, it will still say "both" agree because it is a mutual Agreement. This statement is a very important part of the Agreement, as I described in the last chapter. It should be read with some emphasis and should be in all-caps and/or boldface on your hard copies and in the e-mail copy that you send to him, if he is online. If you have a color printer, it would be good to print it in red ink and to use a large type font so that it stands out.

Part III

Part III is about what you both agree not to *do*. It is about seriously damaging verbally abusive *behaviors* that are not specifically defining of the other person. You can see many in the sample Agreement and in Appendix A. Choose any that you experience. Here are some verbally abusive behaviors that are not *specifically* defining of the partner:

Neither person will:

- Make unilateral decisions. These are decisions that involve both persons but are made by only one person. They jeopardize the other person's freedom to choose, to act, to perceive, or even to think.
- Threaten the other. This is a promise to harm the other person. It is coercive and blocks a person's freedom to act, to know, to choose, and is against human rights.
- Interrogate the other. Interrogation is a series of questions designed to be so rapid they prevent the partner from being able to complete a thought. This form of verbal abuse blocks the recipient's ability to think. And, it implies that the partner is nonexistent.

A list of threats is in Appendix A, on page 244. As none of the lists is complete, if you experience some other abuses that, while not defining you, jeopardize your freedom to act, to think, or to be informed, be sure to include them in Part III.

Part IV

Part IV is about what both parties agree *to* do, and that is, primarily, to relate to each other. There is no relationship if there is no exchange between two people. A relationship between two people is a connection based upon an exchange of information and feedback. Part IV also includes such issues as keeping agreements, asking and responding with "please" and "thank you," asking engaging questions, and responding with understanding.

Part V

Part V is about how both parties agree to *respond* if the Agreement is broken. Since explaining yourself does *not* bring understanding or change in a verbally abusive man, the best response is one that helps him to hear his irrational remarks or to see his irrational behavior. Therefore, if you've heard verbal abuse and tried to explain what bothers you, or what you do know—if, for instance he says, "You don't know what you're talking about"—I recommend that you stop explaining, stop wasting energy and time, and simply ask your mate to repeat what he said. Ask, "What?" or "What did you say?" or "What are you doing?" as stated in the Agreement. In this way, he has a chance to hear his verbally abusive comment, and it may wake him up to his behavior. The more he repeats it, the more you can ask him what he said. Eventually, it may dawn on him that you cannot respond to irrational statements, or give them any validity at all. Bottom line, they are nonsense.

WRITING THE AGREEMENT

As you write up the Agreement and prepare your lists, please keep in mind that the verbally abusive man, to whom you are planning to present the Agreement, may indulge in only a dozen of the approximately four hundred verbally abusive comments I've listed in Appendix A. This does not mean that he is less abusive than someone who indulges in 100 of them. It only means that he is less varied in his ways of denying what he is doing, or silencing you, or venting anger on you, or forming confabulations for his anger and that he is much more covert than the overt, name-calling, swearing verbal abuser. There are more ways of being defined listed in the Appendix. Use only those that apply to your relationship.

If you've already left the relationship, here is a sample of what you might write with the Agreement that you leave behind for your abusive partner.

"In order to know why I left, please note that it is because I heard you tell me what I am, what I do, what I know, what I feel, etc., as per the following, and I tired of hearing you pretend to be me and know what I am, etc."

Sample Agreement

Part I

In order to have a relationship (or a better relationship), both of us with a good and open heart agree that neither will tell the other [fill in your own words and phrases here]:

You are (for example): stupid, too sensitive, a bitch, crazy, selfish, hard to get along with, jumping to conclusions, the one with the problem, too impetuous

You're doing this (for example): attacking me, making a big deal out of nothing, being emotional, blowing it out of proportion, not listening, doing it all wrong, nagging, overreacting, making me mad, pissing me off

You're not doing this (for example): listening to me, trying, being cooperative, doing your share

You must (for example): fix yourself, get off my back, get over it, grow up, quit yakking, shut up, submit to me, do what you're told or else

You should (for example): do it this way, have known better, know what I need

You are trying to (for example): start a fight, be right, get attention, have the last word, win, control me

You feel (for example): too much, sorry for yourself, angry

You (for example): don't feel that way, don't love me, enjoy arguing, don't care, are not upset

You know (for example): what I meant

You don't know (for example): anything, what you're talking about, how good you have it, how to take a joke, what feeling bad really means

You need (for example): to learn to keep a clean house, to toughen up, to get therapy

You think (for example): that I don't know what you're up to, that I am wrong, that I'm going to screw up, that people like you, that you know it all

You want (for example): to have the last word, to be right, to embarrass me, to argue, to win

You have (for example): to be right, everything you could want, bad taste, a problem, issues, to have the last word, no sense of humor

You take things (for example): all wrong, too far, out of context

Your perception (for example): is wrong; you're wrong; it wasn't that way; it didn't happen

Additionally, neither person will define the other through implication or insinuation:

You don't cooperate (for example): When are you going to do your part in this marriage?

You aren't realistic (for example): Let's get down to reality and out of La La Land.

Part II

We agree to the above because neither person is the other nor lives within the other and so cannot know what the other is, thinks, feels, is doing, and so forth.

Part III

Neither person will:

- *Violate the Agreement* by e-mails, notes, or phone messages
- *Disguise abuse as a question* by prefacing any of the abusive statements in Part I with a question by saying, for example: "I don't see why you're so . . ."; "I can't believe you . . ."; "I'm surprised that you . . ."; "I don't mean to say you're . . . but . . ."; "I am not trying to tell you that you don't . . . but . . . ."
- *Define the other as nonexistent* by walking away while the other is talking
- *Make unilateral decisions* by saying, for example: "We're leaving now." "There's nothing to talk about." "We're switching banks." "I've invested the money, so forget it."
- *Deny the above abuses* by saying, for example: "It was just a joke." "Where's your sense of humor?"
- *Blame the other* for the abuse by saying, for example: "If you hadn't . . . then I wouldn't . . ." "It's all your fault."
- *End a conversation* by diverting with a statement like, "I don't want to fight."
- *Interrupt the other* on the phone unless there is a real serious emergency
- *Intimidate the other* by, for example: yelling at the other, raging at the other, getting up close in the other person's face, shaking a finger at the other, blocking the other from leaving the room

- *Threaten the other* by saying, for example: "I could O.J. you." "If you leave, you'll never see the kids again." "I'll make sure you're penniless." "I'll make you sorry."
- *Demonstrate violence* by, for example: throwing things, hitting things, breaking things
- *Be violent* by, for example: restraining, grabbing, shoving, hitting the other
- *Involve the children* in the relationship, nor defame the other to the children, nor stalk the other through the children

Part IV

Both persons agree to:

- *Be bonded together against the problem of verbal abuse.*
- *Look at the other* while the other is speaking.
- *Ask engaging questions*, for example: "How are you feeling?"
- *Respond* to the other with understanding, empathy, and kindness.
- *Excuse themselves* if they can't talk at the moment.
- *Repeat a statement when asked* because the other did not hear.
- *Ask* with a "please" and accept with a "thanks" or "thank you."
- *Take turns* in choosing, for example: movies, restaurants, vacation destinations.
- *Share decisions* about, and control of, joint assets.
- *Ask for what he or she wants.*
- *Tell the other what he or she doesn't want.*
- *Abide by this Agreement*, not only regarding each other, but also with regard to the children.

Part V

Both persons agree that if either person hears the other define them in any way, or sees the Agreement broken, or hears something they are not sure of, that person will say any of the following:

- "What?"
- "What did you say?"
- "What are you doing?"

This will give the other party the opportunity to respond:

- "I meant to say . . ."

And, both agree that if they ask a question and do not hear an answer, they will repeat the question. The exception is if the other asks for clarification; for instance, "Do you mean pick up *our* kids, or our kids and our neighbor's kids?"

If either person breaks the Agreement and hears the other person say, "What?" he or she will apologize and restate what was said in a better way—one that is supportive. The person who did the defining will take back what was said, or if unable to recall what was said, ask, "What did I say?" They might then say, "I take that back. This is what I meant to say . . ." or something similar, or will apologize and be respectful.

And both parties agree to walk away from interrogation if the interrogator does not stop when he or she hears, "What are you doing?"

_____   _____

Signature   *Date*

_____   _____

Signature   *Date*

The partner then invites her mate to add to the Agreement, as it is a mutual undertaking, and asks him to meet with her in a few days (one week maximum) to finalize and sign it. She can remind him that she will have presented it to him in four ways—reading it to him, giving him a hard copy, giving him the tape recording of the Agreement, and e-mailing it to him—so he can add any examples or items he wishes.

A CONVERSATION WITH THE VERBALLY ABUSIVE MAN

The sample questions that follow may help to further wake up the verbally abusive man once he has signed the Agreement. These questions help a man who is, to put it simply, very unaware, or, as I say in *Controlling People*, very "spell bound" and unable to withdraw his dream woman from his partner. If you decide to use the questions or similar ones of your own, then simply say, "I was wondering, do you ever . . . ?" (This alone is a sign of your separateness, that you are not of one mind with him, that you actually do wonder about him.) Then when you are dining with him or having a conversation, bring one up now and then, but only one at a time. And accept whatever he says, unless it is abusive. (In that case, say, "What?")

1. Do you ever think that I should be thinking what you're thinking?

If he says, "yes," tell him that you are probably thinking something different from him most of the time. If he later tells you what you are thinking, say "What?" to remind him that you don't think what he thinks.

If he says "no," say something like, "Good, I'm glad, because I'm not usually thinking what you're thinking."

2. Can you tell me what you're thinking when you just sit and stare at me?

If he tells you, "fine," or he says he doesn't know or isn't thinking anything, you can certainly tell him if you feel uncomfortable when he does that and ask that he try to limit this behavior.

3. Do you feel unloved when I am busy with family or friends on the phone?

If he says, "yes," then simply say that you are sad for him about that, but even so, there will always be times when you will be involved with other people. (Possibly he will learn to grieve his losses, feel his sadness, and not hide his feelings under anger.)

If he says, "no," then say something like, "I'm glad to hear that."

4. Are there times you would like to have more time with me but are hesitant to ask?

If he says, "Yes, you'll say you're too busy," or something similar, say, "What?" He is defining your future. If he says, "I think you'll say . . ." say, "oh," and ask him to please let you know when he would like to make a date with you to do something together.

If he says "no," then that is fine.

5. Do you try daily to be kind and nurturing to me?

If he diverts from the question, for example, "Don't you notice?" or, "I shouldn't have to tell you," or "Why should I?" ask the question again, according to the Agreement. As sweetly and as kindly as possible, ask, "Sweetheart, do you attempt daily to be kind and nurturing to me?"

6. Do you try daily to be kind and nurturing to yourself?

He may ask what you mean, in which case, you would answer his question, explaining what you mean.

7. If you have a negative thought about me like, "She doesn't care," do you change it to a positive thought?

Listen to his answer. He may not know what he thinks, but he may realize in the future that if he does think negatively, it is time to change his thought to a positive one.

8. Do you know that there are things that you can say and do that will draw me closer to you and that there are things you can say and do that will push me away?

This may be something he just wants to think about.

9. Do you believe you have to be perfect?

If the verbally abusive man believes that he has to be perfect, he may be inclined to have a perfect dream woman, perfect children, and a perfect house. He may be angry because the movie in his mind of the perfect world he has concocted is constantly opposed by reality itself. Reality becomes a kind of threat, as does his partner's true personhood. Hence, in time, the verbally abusive man who feels he must be perfect may become not only angrier but also somewhat paranoid.

10. Do you feel anxiety at times?

When the world and particularly his partner are not under his control, the verbally abusive man may feel anxious or panicky.

11. If you feel anxiety, what gives you the most anxiety?

Even if he doesn't answer this question, at least it may lead the verbally abusive man to notice his inner world.

12. Do you feel depressed at times?

Life is difficult if one has been disconnected from their true self and connected instead to a dream person. Depression is a natural outcome, and life is difficult anyway.

13. What do you believe angers you the most?

He may say something about his job or something about a political situation or other innocuous topic. If, however, he says that he gets angry when "you try to pick a fight," "act like you know it all," or some other defining statement, you should be prepared to say, "What did you say?"

14. If our conversations were on video, do you think that they would bring you clarity and understanding about the problems in our relationship?

You may then suggest that you videotape conversation once a week.

15. Do you wonder how I feel when you don't respond to me?

This question may remind him that you are a person and do have feelings.

16. How do you express your love?

He may say something like, he goes to work and provides for his family, or keeps up the yard, or helps move heavy furniture before painting the room.

In the next chapter, we will hear from men who have read something about verbal abuse, and although they have not all seen the Agreement, they are looking for ways to change and are expressing their determination, their struggle, and their chagrin that they have not behaved quite as well as they had thought.

11

MEN SEEKING CHANGE

"I AM GRATEFUL FOR EACH day I choose not to behave that way."

If, before seeing the Agreement, the verbally abusive man comes to the realization that, in fact, he has indulged in verbal abuse, he will know at least to some degree what he has done, and he may know why. But change is rarely easy.

Like many men who read one of my books, one man said, "I can't get over how difficult it is to break this cycle. Thirty years of thinking one way is not something that will go away overnight."

Defining women is so old and pervasive an evil that many men don't notice when it's happening. Recognizing that he has indulged in verbal abuse is the first step for the man quoted above and for all men who are verbally abusive. But even this first step is difficult. For instance, another reader told me, "When I read *Controlling People*, it was as if somebody had written my biography. Maybe not to the extent of some of the people, but I kept thinking, 'She is right. I've done this, this, this, etc.'"

Another man recognized his verbal abuse and wrote to me, "At the request of my wife, I have just begun to read *The Verbally Abusive Relationship* and want to thank you for writing it. You will probably find this compliment a little strange when I tell you that I am discovering that I have been a verbal abuser to my family for years!"

Though these men were willing to look at the problem, they still needed the means to facilitate change, and they could not change overnight. With the aid of the Agreement, they will see how to apply their knowledge to their everyday behavior. If he agrees and signs it, the verbally abusive man will see what he has resolved not to do. Knowing what he has done, however, and what he has resolved not to do, is not enough. Here is a case in point, taken, with his consent, from a letter sent to me by a verbally abusive man:

"I am in a relationship with an amazing woman, whom I want to spend the rest of my life with, but I keep pushing her away and controlling her. I have done this before in other relationships, and I know it isn't right. I just can't figure out why I do it. Sometimes I don't even recognize I am doing it; other times I know it and feel guilty about it afterwards, but I've rarely apologized.

"I have always known something was wrong with the way I behaved and I have never been happy with myself, but I never truly understood the effects of what I was/am doing until my partner read *The Verbally Abusive Relationship* and asked me to read it. My childhood was exactly as you described—verbally abused with no witness—and I now recognize that I am guilty of Discounting, Countering, Withholding, Blocking, Accusing and Blaming, Name Calling, and Denial. I am guilty of this not only in my relationship, but also on a lesser level in my relationships with friends and coworkers. I don't understand why I do this, as I don't feel like it is a power thing, yet I know for a fact I am doing these things. Fortunately, I now see the difference between how I am feeling and how I react. I am hopeful that in the short term I can make better choices for my reactions until I can get a handle on why I feel this way.

"It may be too late to save my relationship, but I need to understand why I can't feel emotions like other men, and work towards being a more complete person. I had gone to a therapist explaining my anger and abusiveness only to have him tell me this was normal in a relationship. I now see that this was very bad advice. I need to talk to someone who knows what he or she is talking about and will hold me accountable.

"Your book has been an unbelievable eye-opener for me. I actually cried. The therapist's response validated that what I was doing was OK and actually made things worse. I know your book was intended for victims of the abuse, but I want to thank you for writing this book as it helped me understand that what I am doing *isn't* normal and it isn't healthy. Up to this point, I thought 'venting' was normal and healthy in a relationship."

MEN LOOKING FOR HELP

Like the men I've quoted in this chapter, more and more men who have been verbally abusive are coming to the realization that they have defined their partners and that they must develop beyond their irrational dependent position. They are seeking change.

One caller, who exemplifies many of the men who indulge in verbally abusive, controlling behaviors, said, "I believe I may often be abusive. I have a somewhat better understanding of what verbal abuse is, but would like to know more about how to become less verbally abusive."

Another said, "I'm not a victim of verbal abuse. I happen to be somebody who is guilty of verbal abuse, running my mouth when I get angry, saying things I don't mean. I've been able to come to the terms that I have a serious problem and I need help; the problem is I keep running into block walls everywhere I go trying to find out where to start to get help."

Let's look at some of their thoughts, insights, and struggles because in doing so, we see that their illusionary view of themselves as loving spouses, or significant others, juxtaposed to their actual behavior is astounding. And, it's astounding to them also! By seeing what is going on with the verbally abusive man, the steps I recommend for change will make more sense. In other words, each recommendation plays a role in implementing his change—his waking up and his integration of his lost self, that which I call his dream woman.

The verbally abusive man who recognizes his indulgence in verbal abuse wants to change not only to become the rational person he wants to be but also to have a real relationship. He also sees that he will need to change from deep within. Realizing the depth of the problem, one man said, "As I learn more about this 'person' I have been, I just don't want to be that person anymore. The worst part about this whole mess I've created is that I have been this way for so long. I truly am anxious to move forward in rehabilitating both my reactions and my thought processes." Another man said, "My previous growth attempts were bogged down by, perhaps, not yet having enough key knowledge of what to change."

On the other hand, some verbally abusive men have not had the opportunity to read, or have refused to read, or have rejected what they've read, about verbal abuse. They aren't ready to recognize themselves through reading or through what their partners have tried so far. These men do best starting with the Agreement. If they receive it before they even hear the words *verbal abuse*, there is a good chance that they will wake up to their behavior. Once they do, they usually want more information and tools to implement the changes they want to make.

In summary, by the time he has seen and signed the Agreement, the verbally abusive man will know what he says and what he has resolved not to do, but he will not yet know how he can break the pattern of verbal abuse. The program I lay out in the next chapter is designed to do just that.

MEN MAKING PEACE WITH CHANGE

Seeking change and the means to change, one man expressed his commitment in the following letter. I am most appreciative of his heartfelt and eloquent expression. He wrote,

"I am a Controller, and I cannot live this way any longer. I just realized what I have been doing. And why, and how I had created a dream woman, just as you said. Your description of how this happened mirrored my life experiences. I am in the middle of therapy and taking an anger management class, but now that I know about what I have been doing, my eyes have begun to open. The walls of my world and the floor on which I stood have crumbled. Now I stand on firmer ground and I see things in a different way, in a brighter light. Although I am sure this will be a life commitment, not to be that way again, to keep my eyes and mind away from that behavior and thinking pattern. At least I see the light at the end of this very dark and heavy tunnel—heavy it has been, losing the love and respect of those I thought I loved, even my own children whom I love dearly, all because of my own behavior.

"And now, now I am in the midst of struggling to really see and hear my wife, for she means the world to me. The difference is, I no longer want to turn her into my 'dream woman,' I just want to share my life with her, and her to share with me. I want to appreciate, not control, her experience, nor define her reactions, nor expect certain reactions. I needed to let you know. And I still have a way to go, but want to thank you for having given a tool to those who are lost in controlling people, as well as those witnesses who need to get out of this persecution.

"Having been so controlling, I want to say that being that way is exhausting not only to the witness, but to the controller as well, always vigilant to see if the other, the object of my control, will make a mistake, never trusting, always with a doubt. But again, I say thank you for opening my eyes and my heart. My emotions are raw from feeling things, emotions, but at least I am getting to see things in the right direction and not backwards."

Other men, too, have shared their insights, and remarkably, they too say, in so many words, "being that way is exhausting."

The following note is from a man describing how he struggled to overcome his partner's boundaries. He wrote:

"Imagine the paradox. She was setting boundaries and I was stuck in pretend world, not yet aware of how it worked. As you might guess, it was a disaster. She was very hurt that her boundaries were so disrespected by me even though she practically spray-painted her rules on the wall. I was very much outside in, trying desperately to keep my wife from leaving me, in a crippled mindset that was futile and irrational. As I was getting the opposite results of what I prayed for, I turned up the fire and more intensely attempted to salvage my marriage. I was *exhausted* from the grip of pretend world and she was also exhausted.

"For the first time that I can remember, I realized that I was treating her as an extension of myself all this time and I didn't even know it. It's like I was watching someone else ruin my married life. But I can see how being the super controller has dictated my thoughts and caused me to try to define her reality for her in order to keep her close. And that's been very painful for her. I'm grimacing at how often she has had to second-guess herself as to why I could not, would not, hear her beg to be recognized."

Yet another man shared his insights with me.

"The intense argument my wife and I had over her trying to get me to read your book almost ended our marriage. Ironically, her suggestion turned into a huge power struggle between us, a power struggle over reading a book about the misuse of power. The fight we had was brutal, but I did read the book, slowly and consciously. I felt like a 100-pound weight had been lifted off my shoulders that I had been carrying around all of my life. I now understood a piece of myself that had kept me alone, angry, and suffering all my life. I felt like God had breathed life into me, that life was in fact perfect, there was a plan, and I was supported and loved after all.

"I was raised by a colonel in the Marine Corps. I grew up as a jock, the definitive Alpha Male. Power by domination was my creed, and no one could match, challenge, or discern my innate ability to undermine, manipulate, and control until Feb. 15, 2004. I had always marveled at my ability to dominate any person or situation—no one anywhere was as powerful as me, I thought. Then I learned what I always knew deep inside, that I had no power at all, in fact I was desperately powerless. My self-loathing I could accept; after all, I had lived with it for forty years and people revered me as an evolved, highly conscious, spiritual teacher. I was loved by everyone. But, I could not support a woman (my wife) whom I truly loved. I was threatened by her and needed to continuously keep her small, less than me, so that I could feel big.

"As this began to reveal itself to me, I knew something was deeply wrong. Your work was the bridge. As a teacher myself I often wonder if we really do make a difference, or is it all illusion? Now I know the answer. Your book, your compassionate message to the world, changed my life. As I said, I am a spiritual teacher, working with couples and primarily with men. Your book is now my bible. Being an expert at this behavior myself, I can spot the dynamic in anyone and help women to understand and men to have greater compassion for themselves. You can be sure that as I am out in the world teaching, your gifts are being shared with every person I meet, especially the men, and your light and vision continue to shine, heal, open, and touch many lives.

"And for me, any time I am in judgment in any way, I know that at that moment I am feeling powerless. I go inside, breathe, feel my feelings, and thank God for my humanness and love myself a little more. I don't know you, Ms. Evans, but my wish to you is that you can allow yourself to fully receive the impact of my e-mail to you, my expression of gratitude, awe, and open-hearted love. You are an angel; may your life continue to be blessed."

While one man believes that he must watch every word he speaks so that he won't accidentally say something defining of his wife, another says, "I have found that if you try to let go with your head, you will screw it up every time. But if you let go with your heart, even though it is a thousand times harder to do, you will do and say the right thing every time." He is right. People often equate feelings with heart. In the story of Dorothy in Oz, we see that the Tin Man needed a heart because he wasn't in touch with his feelings. In fact, he was afraid that if he shed a tear, he might become immobilized with rust and nearly die.

To many men, expressing their feelings is tantamount to death, as certainly is the feeling of death that comes from losing father acceptance, especially when that acceptance depends on not showing one's feelings. Letting go of the dream woman, withdrawing her from his partner, means that she cannot be his feeling part. She is not his emotional self. He must develop his own feeling self, and thus draw the energy out of his dream woman. Like the Tin Man, he has to have a heart. Letting go of the dream woman and feeling his own feelings, is, as this man says, a thousand times harder to do than to just let go with your head.

IT IS NOT ENOUGH

It is not enough for the verbally abusive man to know that he has been living in a dream state, with an unlived self, personified as a dream woman anchored in his partner. His knowing does not dissolve his dream woman.

It is not enough for him to want to be different more than anything. He needs to know what to do because wanting to change without direction, without a plan for change, would not effect change.

A man who indulges in verbal abuse and is capable of change needs the tools required to do the work of change. Imagine the partner is with a man who says, "I won't tell you what you are, what you think, what you mean, because I don't live within you," and he agrees to stop when he hears "What?" Then he tries for a while to control himself—for instance, by going to an anger management program—but without the tools he needs, he may explode one day saying, "I can't do this! I'm out of here!"

It is important that he know that *change is not a matter of will alone. The verbally abusive man must have a multifaceted plan to implement the change he seeks.* And he has to be willing to say, "I have a problem and need more support, more help, more therapy, or whatever."

It is not enough for him to want to change in order to get back his partner. Change would not be real or permanent if it were entirely dependent on getting back the body that harbors his dream woman. In fact, to be changed he would have to do the work and then be so changed that he supports his partner in whatever she wants to do, including not being with him, if that is her choice. That would be real change. Wanting her back is usually only his first motive for even looking at changing. As he begins doing the work of changing—reading, therapy, and so forth—if he realizes that he has been irrational and hurtful he will be motivated to change so as to become a healthier person.

It is not realistic for him to gauge his progress by his partner's warmth and appreciation of him. She is not likely to say, "You're so wonderful for not abusing me." If he uses her warmth and appreciation as a gauge, he is not seeing her as a separate person. As a separate person, she may be recovering from countless traumas. She may be afraid he might abuse again. She may still be walking on eggshells. She may just not like him anymore. She may have lost all desire for him because he has not been a friend or protector of her since she can remember. She may not feel emotionally safe with him. And as if that were not enough, she may not have felt seen or heard by him for a very long time.

He would need to know very clearly, at least at a conceptual level, that the core of the problem is his dream woman, the unlived self. If he were to change, he would need to integrate his unlived self to a great extent. He would need to practice relating to his partner as if she really were a separate person. He would need to approach the problem from many angles.

Now that the Agreement has awakened him to his behavior and we have seen his desire to change, these are the steps I invite him to take.

12

THE PROCESS OF CHANGE

MANY MEN WHO HAVE AGREED not to indulge in verbal abuse are desperate to change, as we saw by comments in the last chapter. This chapter will support the change they seek, giving them many approaches to recover themselves, and thus dissolve the dream woman. If you are with a man who promises to change, you can tell him that this is the chapter that will show him what he can do to begin the work.

Agreeing not to define each other is a fine thing to do, but there is much more work to be done. This chapter will show the abuser the many things he can do to heal and integrate his unlived self, which holds all the qualities and functions he could not develop and which were arrested in their development. These things include making lists and what these lists are about, journal writing, the kind of therapy that would be helpful and the goal of that therapy, planned meetings with his partner, and so on. All are important to facilitate his change.

Now that he has signed the Agreement and he knows that either person will say, "What?" if they see it broken, he may notice that keeping the Agreement may be very difficult. If the verbally abusive man has agreed to abide by the Agreement to the best of his ability, he will have realized that there are things he has said that are not okay and that are hurtful to his partner. He may also have some realization that he says them because he is acting as if he knows his partner's inner reality. These realizations don't really change him, but they are the foundation of change. Like a house, the foundation has to be there before anything can be built upon it. As far as his relationship is concerned, it can only be built by the work he puts into it.

To facilitate change, men who have consulted with me have found the following suggestions useful:

1. Think of your partner as a best friend, not an enemy. How would you treat a best friend? This idea helps men to see their partners as real people. One man shared with me, "The sad part is we never talked. We seemed to have a better relationship before we were married and were just friends."

2. Hold your partner in the context of curiosity. That is, know that you cannot assume anything about her, ever. This helps many men realize that they may hold assumptions; for instance, "I'm happy, so she is happy." Or, "I prefer that people look the other way if I get tears in my eyes, so she must want me to turn my back to her when she is crying over a family loss."

3. Ask yourself several times a day, "Am I being kind to her and others?" If men have trouble knowing what is kind, I suggest that they ask their partners.

4. Be solicitous of her feelings, listen to her, and acknowledge her. It is likely that whatever she is feeling unhappy about is

something that she has heard her mate say, or seen him do, and it is likely that she has not said or done the same thing to sadden him. Another man shared with me his insights after his partner left him. She felt unheard and unseen by him, and once she left, he began to realize that he had not really understood her. "I never realized how unconscious I was of her feelings. I was always there for her when it came to other people and any associated pain she felt but seemed to not be able to recognize when I was the one causing her pain. The pain I caused her was by not listening, plain and simple. I was always there for our children in every way but was never able to give her the nurturing she needed. She would say, 'Why can't you talk to me nicely like you do to the kids?' I don't know if I felt nurturing stops when you grow up or what."

5. Be patient, especially if she is wounded, sad, or busy and not feeling affectionate. If you make the assumption that an X number of months have gone by so she should be thanking you for not abusing her, and she should feel safe with you, and she should desire you, you are talking about your dream woman.

6. Know that your partner will not usually feel affectionate toward you until she feels emotionally safe with you. This feeling of safety is not something she can conjure up, and conversely, she cannot make a feeling of apprehension disappear.

THE PARTNER'S JOB

But just as your mate will have work to do, so will you. Your work will be, primarily, to say "What?" or "What are you doing?" if he breaks the Agreement or, if he tries to divert from answering a question, to repeat the question as appropriate. It is likely that your mate will occasionally break the Agreement because changing a pattern and way of being with one's partner is not easy. Although it is to be expected that the verbally abusive man will lapse and his partner will need to respond to that lapse, it is difficult for most partners to simply say, "What?" This is so because they automatically react as if their mate were rational and would understand an explanation or defense against an accusation or other verbally abusive comment. I have suggested to the partners of verbally abusive men that when they wake in the morning, they say a little mantra, "What? What? What?" so that it becomes more automatic than explaining in case they hear verbal abuse.

The following approaches to change are designed to help the verbally abusive man see his partner and family members as separate people. Also, they are meant to help him become acquainted with his own emotional self and his own inner world. By doing the work outlined below, he has a 95 percent, or better, chance of changing. But, if he only reads about it and forgets to do it, change is not likely.

Whether he begins with reading, writing in a notebook, or finding a trauma therapist, the point is that he does all the steps that he can do, together, not sequentially. In other words, his schedule might look like this: getting up twenty minutes earlier and writing in his journal, reading during lunch break, seeing a trauma therapist Saturday morning, practicing conversation with his partner after dinner, attending an anger management program on Tuesday and Thursday evenings, saving Sunday evening for special conversation with his partner, and mentally practicing affirmations all the while. In summary, the program is an intensive learning and integrating time in his life. I suggest a number of approaches to change, and, like vitamins taken together, they work synergistically. Each makes the other more effective.

READING ABOUT CONTROL AND VERBAL ABUSE

Along with the recommendations that follow in this chapter, the person seeking change within himself must become knowledge-able about what has brought about his indulgence in verbal abuse and the impact his behavior has had on his family. By under-standing how he has created a dream partner, and possibly dream children, he can focus on change and can know just what about himself needs to change. I recommend a half hour or more of reading per day, until he has read my four previous books on verbal abuse and control[9], then at least ten minutes a day for the following year. He should continue reviewing and reading any other books he finds helpful for every week thereafter.

ANGER MANAGEMENT

An anger management program brings some awareness to men who are angry and gives them some tools to control their anger. I recommend that the overtly verbally abusive man—that is, one who yells, rages, or shows smoldering anger—attend an anger manage-ment program, in addition to reading, journaling, and attending the specific therapy that I explain in this chapter. The anger man-agement program is an adjunct to the complete program.

Anger management plays a role in recovery. It is like put-ting an ointment on a rash. The symptom is reduced, so one has time to look for the cause, which is yet to be discovered. For example, the anger is managed but its underlying cause is not often addressed. Some anger management programs recommend that attendees read my book *Controlling People* so they under-stand about their dream woman and about their need to keep her viable at the expense of the real woman's consciousness.

Very few men, however, change solely by being in an anger management program because they do not know the source of their anger. Men who indulge in verbally abusive behaviors toward their partners may learn to manage their anger, or refrain from verbally abusive comments for a time, but their anger, whether expressed covertly or overtly, and their need to ignore the real woman, is still there. That is the problem. Managing the symptom, anger, is fine and may even save lives, but knowing what is behind abusive behaviors in relationships, and addressing the cause, is required for real change to take place.

The only man I know who really changed through his participation in an anger management program said that he attended it for eight years, and that it was only after the first three years that he began to honestly acknowledge his problems and begin the hard work of reorganizing, integrating, and processing his own traumatic and painful past. If a man attends for say, six months, or only occasionally over the course of a year, the program is not at all likely to be effective. Until the verbally abusive man learns what is wrong and recognizes his unlived, unintegrated self (known to us as the dream woman), he doesn't know why he is angry, particularly at his partner and those closest to him. Managing anger is not the solution, but it is an important part of the solution.

THERAPY

Besides reading about the problem of verbal abuse and his need to keep his dream woman alive and well in his partner, and his managing his anger at the real woman for actually showing up where his dream woman was supposed to be, I recommend that the verbally abusive man find a therapist who will work with him in recovering his unlived self. If he is among those who can change, I believe that it is by knowing what happened to him and how it impacted him, and then healing from it, that he is able to change. I suggest that as he interviews a therapist to find the right person for him, he would tell him or her that his goal is to integrate the experiences he had when he was young because they are still affecting him. The goal is that the therapist help him through the traumas and experiences of childhood so that he can reintegrate what he could not process or integrate in his early years. These are the emotions, functions, and experiences that were left in his unconscious to form a dream woman, or even a dream family. In therapy, reintegrating his emotional self, and learning what verbal abuse is and how it has impacted him can help to release him from the trap of being a verbal abuser himself.

If he was abused constantly, as was Hitler by his father, his unlived self would be so huge he could have a dream world, as did Hitler.[10] On the other hand, he may recall a happy childhood and no abuse at all. Or, as is common, he may simply not recall anything before the age of nine or ten. Some men recall being physically abused but have convinced themselves that they deserved the abuse.

Babette Rothschild, LCSW, author of *The Body Remembers: The Psychophysiology of Trauma and Trauma Treatment* (W.W. Norton & Company, 2000), advises those seeking trauma therapy to thoroughly explore the smorgasbord of therapies and therapists available in their community. Even though there is a lot of competition between trauma therapy models, research continues to show that it is the therapeutic relationship that is the most central in successful treatment. As well as paying attention to the therapist's education, professional manner, and general philosophy, she suggests picking one who can draw from at least three methods so that there can be ample flexibility.

Rothschild also cautions that all responsible trauma therapists will first determine whether working with abuse memories is the best tack for the client now or in the future, suggesting alternatives if it is not. If trauma memories are approached inappropriately or prematurely, there could be risks to the person's well-being. Hesitant to recommend particular therapies, she believes it is really a matter of taste, what appeals to an individual—both therapist and client—emphasizing that there are many, many good methods available. She suggests a thumb-through *The Body Remembers Casebook* (W.W. Norton & Company, 2003) where she demonstrates a dozen methods she has found useful, including but not limited to Somatic Trauma Therapy, Somatic Experiencing, EMDR, Gestalt Therapy, Transactional Analysis, and Cognitive Behavioral Therapy. She believes, however, that it is really the ability to tailor a therapy to the unique needs of each client, drawing from a multitude of methods, combined with a good emotional and intellectual fit between therapist and client, that will lay the foundation for a successful therapy.

In any case, I recommend trauma therapy that can address a man's childhood experiences. In therapy, the man who wants change can find out about experiences he had as a child and how they impacted him, even when he blocked them off as they occurred. He can find out how his functions were disabled and how to actually regain awareness of what happened to him.

One of the goals that men set for themselves when they want to integrate or process their experiences, is to research and find a therapist they are comfortable with. Resources are on the Internet.[11] If their experiences were blocked off, then all the feelings and the very character of their traumas would be left in their unconscious, only adding to the energy of their dream woman. And her burden is to make it all better, which is an impossible task.

If verbally abusive men, as adults, are unable to accept their own childhood experiences, they are unable to accept their partners' experiences, and often their children's experiences.

Some men become depressed because of the way they were themselves defined in childhood. People who feel suicidal release a great deal when they know that what they were told about their inner reality, even their future ("You'll never amount to anything.") was a lie. Therapy can help the verbally abusive man to know that just as he cannot define his partner, no one had a right to define him in childhood. The realizations and integrations he can achieve in therapy can help him let go of his need to be right. And he can come to the realization that he still exists after he lets go of his ideal picture and sees himself as a person who can make mistakes.

One man wrote:

"I am one of those controlling men who was raised in a household that was (and still is) based backwards in control relationships. I am looking for professional support to improve my current behavior and interpersonal relationships. I have been involved in therapy and family counseling before, and it would have been *much* more effective if I would have zeroed-in on the root problem that Patricia Evans has written about so clearly."

Anyone dealing with a verbally abusive man, including the partner, benefits from having some understanding of how his dream woman developed and then became anchored in his partner. This understanding is also very helpful to women who have dealt with a verbally abusive man in the past. It is almost an essential for a woman dealing with verbal abuse in the present, and it is just as necessary for anyone working with people who are exploring the impact of verbal abuse in family relationships and even work-related situations. Therapy that addresses childhood training and trauma can be very effective in healing any man who finds he has been abusive.

THE FIVE LISTS

To facilitate reading this section, I will call the man who wants to change, Jack, and his partner, Jill, both of whom we met in the picnic scenario in Chapter 2. To begin the process of learning to address Jill as if she were a real person, Jack would have to go beyond strictly functional communications. Developing and using the lists I suggest will help him in his communications with her and with others.

List 1: Engaging Questions

I recommend that Jack make a list of engaging questions to ask Jill. Engaging questions are questions that actually do just that—they address the other person as if she were, in fact, a separate person. They ask the other person about herself. They aren't questions about things or events, such as, "Is the garbage out?" or "What time does the movie start?" Clients are often surprised to realize that they have failed to address their partners as separate people with questions such as these.

I recommend that Jack not only compose a list of engaging questions and read through them on a daily basis so that the questions and the style of speaking become familiar to him, but also that he add to the list whenever he thinks of another question. As a result, if Jack and Jill are, for example, having dinner together, or riding in their car, they can have a conversation.

Following are some examples of engaging questions.

"How are you?"
"What did you like most about the movie?"
"What is your favorite flower?"
"What do you want to do in retirement?"
"What would you do if you won a lottery?"

"What do you like most about our relationship?"
"What would you like to see change in me?"

If Jack and Jill are separated due to abuse, but meeting occasionally or corresponding by e-mail, Jack's engaging questions could be more explicit. He could acknowledge that he does, indeed, recognize how his behavior impacted her. In this case, his questions would be something like the following:

"Do you feel like you're 'walking on eggshells' when we talk?"
"Are you nervous when you hear my car drive up?"
"Is there anything you want to talk about that bothers you?"
"Do you ever wake up at night worrying about things?"

There could be hundreds of questions in List 1. I recommend that Jack ask at least one or two when he is in conversation with Jill. And, some questions suggest others; for example, "Did you like the movie?" can be followed up with, "What did you like most about it?" Of course, these questions all require understanding or empathetic responses. This leads us to our next list, which is about understanding and empathetic responses.

List 2: Understanding and Empathetic Responses

Not only does Jack need to be able to engage his partner as a separate person, but also he needs to respond to her with understanding if he is going to change within. His understanding and empathetic responses confirm his partner's separateness. After all, prior to change, he would not have been able to respond with empathy to a real woman because he would have feared breaking his connection to his dream woman, who is a large part of himself. Now, by consciously breaking his connection to his dream woman and responding to the real woman, Jack furthers his own growth. He integrates the quality of kindness or empathy that had formerly resided in his dream woman, and he faces his partner as a real person, thereby conditioning himself to her separateness.

I recommend that Jack start a list of empathetic or understanding responses and that he add to it any time he thinks of a new one, and that he review it daily. The list could be in a notebook or in a laptop. What's important is reviewing it, adding to it, and using appropriate responses in conversation. Here are a few examples:

> *"I hear you."*
> *"I heard you say. . . Is that right?"*
> *"I see."*
> *"I understand."*
> *"That's great."*
> *"I am glad to hear that."*
> *"Oh, what a bummer."*
> *"That's cool."*

The verbally abusive man may put forth great effort to grow and change, but he may occasionally forget himself and define his partner when the appropriate response would be to encourage her. For example, Jill's happiness over something she's become interested in may feel threatening to Jack because he suddenly can't find his dream woman. (The dream woman isn't interested in what his partner is interested in.) Maybe Jill wants to take a watercolor class. When she talks about it, Jack says, "That won't get you anywhere," predicting her future.

If he finds he has forgotten himself and defined his partner in some way, he then has to apologize and take back what he said. This leads us to the next list.

List 3: Taking It Back

In the course of conversation, people may tell others what they are, or think, and so forth, but when it is brought to their attention, or even when they suddenly hear themselves, they "take it back"; that is, they apologize and rephrase the statement, saying, "I take that back," or, "I meant to say . . ." This reconstitutes the relationship.

Thus, Jack is engaged in a major project because being able to say, "I was wrong," or "I made a mistake" are some of the statements that some men have never heard another man say. Some men grow up and live in a world of one-upmanship, where exerting power over others is not looked down upon as bullying but admired as winning, and where no one ever admits that they're wrong.

For Jack, there is the possibility that if he can't take it back when he defines his partner, it is the end of his relationship. So, making and using List 3 is very important.

Here are some suggestions to get started. This list, which will not be as long as the others, is still one of the most important lists Jack can make and should include at least a dozen alternatives.

"I take that back."
"I meant to say . . ."
"I am so sorry I said that."
"What I meant to say was . . ."

List 4: Self-Revelation

From our perspective, the verbally abusive man lives under the illusion that he can define the inner world of his partner. Conversely, he seems also to live under the illusion that his partner knows what he thinks and wants—in other words, all about him. In order for Jack to become used to the fact that Jill is separate from him, and is not, therefore, a dream woman, I recommend another list—of personal information—he can share with Jill. The items on the list do not necessarily have to be about specifics. They can include reminders to himself to share his current experiences, thoughts, and feelings. Here is a sample list.

"Something that happened at work today . . ."
"How I feel about an upcoming holiday . . . "
"What I'd like most to do when I retire . . ."
"My favorite subject in high school was . . ."

A person can introduce a self-revelation with a question: "Did I ever tell you what I . . ." While he is sharing himself, he can find a way to travel the path of his growth and change, with his partner, by not only sharing information about himself, his work, his hopes and dreams, but also about what he is learning about himself now—the events that he can see affected him—the experiences that left him so disconnected from himself, so anchored in, and dependent on, his partner.

Like a mantra, I suggest that Jack remind himself that asking, responding, and sharing build a relationship.

List 5: Affirmations

Jack now realizes that his abusive behavior came out of attempts to keep his dream woman alive and present and to disappear or silence the real woman. He can affirm this realization. I recommend that he make a list of affirmations and review and add to it daily. It could include the following:

"I am not my behavior."
"I may say or do something reprehensible, but I can rectify it."
"I am not a horrible person just because I behaved badly."

"I can take my remorse and transform it into determination to act in a respectful and honest way."

This last list and its positive note lead us to a very important part of Jack's recovery program. That is, Jack's continued recovery of his unlived self and the consequent dissolution of his dream woman.

SELF-NURTURANCE

Since Jack was, to a great extent, disconnected from his own inner world and much of his feeling, sensate, and intuitive functions, tuning in to and acknowledging this part of himself is important. He may suppress his natural empathy because it was a quality he didn't see in his father or was not allowed to express.

Many human qualities, including the ability to feel, were wrongly ascribed to the feminine when he was younger. Consequently, Jack suppressed them so he would feel masculine. The consequence, however, was that he could not become fully functional. His inner world and the qualities that all people are born with were lost to him. But they can be found and integrated.

Nurturing himself does not mean that Jack indulges in escape tactics like increased drinking, gambling, etc. To nurture himself is to live a healthy lifestyle. After all, if someone is numbed out on alcohol, they are definitely disconnected and beside themselves. And when the verbally abusive man is "beside himself," he is definitely anchored in his partner. He's not anchored in himself. That's why people get so difficult when they are intoxicated. They are more disconnected from themselves and more intent on making the people around them into dream people who do what they want and think what they think.

Nurturing himself includes eating right and learning about nutrition and exercise. Nurturing himself is getting to know himself and what stresses him and how to deal with that stress. When he is stressed, his disconnection is magnified. He is more "beside himself," just as he would be if he were intoxicated, and he becomes more dependent and is more deeply anchored in his dream woman. In other words, his partner must be his dream woman at all times. His reactions to the real woman are extreme.

Nurturing himself is being sympathetic and empathetic to his own emotional self in order to bring his feeling function back to full capacity. It is a way of parenting one's self, being one's own best father and one's own best mother.

One way to do this would be for Jack to personify his emotional self as his own child within, and then attend to that aspect of himself by thinking of his emotional self as an inner child and addressing the inner child in a nurturing way. He would do this by talking to his own "inner child."

Nearly all men I consult to say that when their relationship is in jeopardy, they feel sad and anxious. An inner dialogue with their inner child might look like this. "How are you feeling?" *I understand.* "Of course, you feel anxious." *I'll take care of you.* "Are you tired?" *Let's rest a while.* "You don't have to push through." *I'll take care of you.* This inner dialogue is far better than calling himself names, telling himself, for instance, "Don't be a wimp."

If he has children, he can also develop his nurturing ability by nurturing and respecting his children's inner world.

As he cares for himself in this way, he is using the nurturing qualities that he couldn't develop because nurturance was not allowed expression, development, or integration in his own childhood.

Jack can tune in to his inner world with something as simple as noticing while driving that he is hungry and deciding to stop to get something to eat, rather than pushing on to make some imagined deadline. In this example, pushing on while ignoring one's needs is often the result of having had a demanding father who told his son to push himself in some pursuit that was beyond his skill at the time. The son internalizes the "You're not good enough" message and, as if to prove the parent wrong, he attempts to disconnect from his experience, to ignore his needs, to reach a destination faster than last time. Consequently, he relegates to his unconscious the quality of nurturance and the ability to take care of himself—even including his awareness of his hunger.

Some men, although chronologically adults, have never learned to take care of themselves—from making a sandwich when they are hungry, to making sure they have clean socks, it is all a mystery. One man in his late forties, told his wife, "It's your job to take care of me." He was not physically disabled. He was well educated with an engineering degree and a good job, but he had never taken care of himself. And he talked to his wife as if she were not a real person, but his dream woman telling her what her job was.

With a more positive outlook, a man who faced divorce said to his partner, "I need to fix myself, so that even if I lose you, I can be better for myself and my children." This man came to grips with verbal abuse, and has every intention of wrestling it to the ground. No more will the specter of a dream woman and dream children descend upon him and cloud his vision. His goal is to see his family as actual, separate people, not lost parts of himself.

Being willing to change for his own well-being, to be a better person, not just to ensure that his wife will stay with him, is the highest form of commitment. It is a commitment to self, to soul, to spirit that moves human consciousness one step forward on the path to consciousness.

When I talk with men such as this one, who are seeking change within themselves, I sometimes ask them, "When was the last time you wept for your childhood? How often did you hear your father say, 'Of course you are scared [of the dark, the boogie man, the mean kid at school]. That's okay. Everything will be alright. I'll take care of you.'?"

And then they cry.

They have the courage to face their pain and begin the process of gaining the capacity to feel empathy for others because they are learning to feel empathy for the child within.

Another benefit of developing the quality of nurturance is that the process takes it out of the dream woman, actualizes it, and integrates it into consciousness, allowing it to develop so that it would not only be integrated, but also used. Jack would have the opportunity while here on planet Earth to actually use those qualities that would otherwise remain dormant and die with him.

I'll never forget a client who was ignored when he was very, very sick as a child. He learned to ignore his physical experience, that is, to disconnect from his sensate function. After a serious accident, he stood up, said "I'm okay," and later found out he had many broken bones. Though his case was extreme, there are many people who cut or bruise themselves, suddenly notice it, and wonder when it happened.

In another case, a man said that when he was thirteen, playing baseball, he swung a bat with a sprained wrist because he felt his father expected him to perform, no matter what. Like most men I consult to, he had learned to suffer while losing awareness of his own experience. These men block out painful injuries, conforming to an unrecognized rule that they be so disconnected from their own experiences, they will take orders and readily go to war. But many others go to war with courage, not with disconnection.

A PERSONAL JOURNAL

Separate from keeping the previous lists, I also recommend that Jack, who is developing more awareness and consequently becoming more conscious of Jill's separateness, keep a personal journal.

He can support himself in his growth, preferably by writing every morning as Julia Cameron recommends in her very fine book *The Artist's Way* (Jeremy P. Tarcher, 1992). This book on journaling recommends writing first thing in the morning to capture the insights, inspirations, and ideas that filter up to consciousness by early morning. By tuning in to what he is feeling, a kind of "looking within," Jack, who is recovering himself, can become more aware of his feelings, his insights, and his experiences. He will also be able to track his progress, and as an added bonus, he will be more in touch with his own creativity. Doing this for himself is another way to take care of himself. And, as he puts caring qualities into action, he will be pulling that energy out of his dream woman, utilizing qualities left stagnant in his own unconscious, and integrating them into consciousness. And, as Jack looks within, he will know what he is doing and be less inclined to tell Jill what she is doing!

Ultimately, through this work, Jack will come to an understanding of how much of himself was left undeveloped to become this huge gestalt of qualities and experiences in his unconscious that, in fact, became personified as a dream woman.

A SACRED CONVERSATION TIME

I recommend that Jack, who is in the process of changing, invite Jill to set aside a special time just to visit with him. As you already know—and I want to emphasize here—conversation involves an exchange between two people, that is, a relationship. Conversation builds a relationship. Setting aside one to three hours a week to talk with each other, to engage and respond to each other in conversation, is essential. A man might change without this exercise, but how will he or his partner know, if he rarely if ever spends a whole hour in conversation with her?

By setting aside a special time to converse with Jill, and actually conversing with her, Jack can practice using the tools of engagement, of responding with understanding, of expressing his thoughts and feelings, and—ultimately and most significantly—of experiencing Jill as a separate person, not his unlived self, his dream woman.

Inviting Jill to meet with him to visit together, possibly on a dinner date, or after dinner at home, will give Jack a chance to communicate, a chance to say "please" and "thank you," and to accept a "no" if Jill doesn't feel emotionally safe with him and isn't ready for a date with him.

Jill, too, may initiate a request for this conversation time. Overall, no matter who initiates it, it is good for both parties to see it as a special time where they can share their lives with each other.

During their sacred communication time, Jack and Jill may, as I suggested in *Controlling People*, keep their own tape recorders turned on and on the table, so that they can play back what they said, just in case they forget themselves.

SOME KEY CONCEPTS FOR THE MAN IN THE PROCESS OF CHANGE

- Verbal abuse, the defining of another person, is irrational.
- Seeing your partner as a separate person acknowledges her existence.
- You are not your partner. You never know why she says what she says.
- Your partner doesn't feel happy just because you feel happy.

- There are things you can say that will bring her closer to you, and there are things you can say that will push her away.

THE IMPORTANCE OF EMPATHY

Without empathy, one cannot really be connected to another person. And one cannot feel empathy for that person unless he or she is perceived as a separate person.

I asked a man, "Did you ever feel empathy or sadness for the situation of someone else?" He said, "The only time I felt sadness like that was when I inadvertently backed the car up over my dog."

Possibly, as he focuses on that time, he can begin to develop a sense of himself as a person who is capable of feeling empathy. As he comes to the realization that he has the capacity to feel for another, he can tune into his feelings of empathy for his partner, but this can only happen if he can see her as a separate person.

Ultimately then, if she says something bothers her, he can ask her about it and feel empathy for her, rather than feel attacked because the real woman has shown up, and he can't find the rest of himself (his dream woman). As he develops self-awareness, he might eventually connect to his partner through empathy rather than in a backward way via his dream woman. He can then give up the struggle to constantly shape her into the image and likeness of his unlived self.

In the next chapter, we will see in a dialogue how the dream woman triangulates a relationship until the real woman disappears from the mind and consciousness of the verbally abusive man.

13

HE WON'T AGREE

FROM OUR PERSPECTIVE, VERBALLY ABUSIVE men assault the minds of women because they have become disconnected from their inner worlds and have anchored their disconnected selves in women. Whether overtly or covertly, consciously or unconsciously, they seek to control the minds and often the bodies of those in whom they have anchored themselves. An abuser who assaults the mind of his partner on a daily basis, as does Jill's abuser, is only so many degrees away from men who assault the minds of women en masse.

I must mention these men who collectively assault the minds of the women around them because by looking at the extreme, we can see why change is so important. Also, seeing what could happen if things went too far will hopefully motivate a man who won't comply with the Agreement. After all, some very good men have lived their lives connected to their partners through a dream woman, having no real comprehension of their having an unlived self, anchored in their partner. They really don't realize how incredibly destructive their behavior is.

By looking at the extreme, we see how the extremist, having more power over his partner than the average verbally abusive man, is doing exactly what the average verbal abuser does, but he is doing it in a radical way. And he is doing it with more social sanction, or despite social sanction, or because social sanctions are not enforced. He is not simply telling his partner (the real woman) what she is, what she thinks, or that what just happened didn't happen in an attempt to erase her mind, empty her of consciousness, silence her, and fill her up with his dream woman. No, the extremist is taking away her mind by preventing its development. It is simply easier for him to anchor the rest of himself in an empty mind than to go through the efforts of brainwashing her with verbal abuse. Despite the many ways there are to erase her mind, he needn't go to the trouble. If he has power, he can keep his partner isolated and uneducated, unable to read or to write, unable to know that women are part of the world and part of humanity, unable to have a mind by simply killing anyone who would educate her. Very simply put, he can succeed in making her into his dream woman, a part of his mind and virtually nothing else.

EXTREMISTS

By observing the defining of women at the extreme, we can see the impact of verbal abuse on both women and men. Some extremists, such as members of the Taliban, succeed in almost totally erasing the real woman. They would never accept an Agreement to be mutual with their partner because they have lost so much of themselves and depend on their partners to personify their lost selves. Though the abuse of women is against Afghan law, the law does not deter the extremists. These men appear to be as disconnected as would be a psychological quadriplegic; that is, they are disconnected from their emotions, unable to feel empathy for others; disconnected from their sensate function, willing to be part of mayhem; disconnected from their intuitive function, unable to anticipate their failure to ever really achieve their purpose; and disconnected from their humanity, having no conscience and no remorse.

En masse, men like these agree to eradicate the minds of women by isolating them from the world and from education—after all, it's so much easier to control a person who cannot read or write. But how can this be done? By killing teachers who educate girls, of course. One such horrifying event occurred in January 2006 in a central Afghan town.[12] Since the teacher's eight children and his wife were forced to watch his beheading, this violence will certainly go a long way in the silencing of the real woman. One might imagine that not many girls will be in school in that area in the future, and it will be very hard to find a teacher for a coeducational school.

The Taliban's efforts to keep the rest of themselves alive in the bodies, minds, and souls of the women whose consciousness they annihilate brought about this atrocity. Since they don't know about the missing parts of themselves, their unlived selves, their dream women, they attribute their unconscionable actions to religion. They say that they are purists following Islam, as if to say that God is behind their horrifying violence. This is their not so subtle attempt to sanctify their evil behavior and is terrifying to women all over the world. At the time of the teacher's beheading, less than one percent of the students attending school there were female.[13] The Taliban's threats and their assaults have kept real women in the dark. Their attacks and murders are hate-crimes—though not directed at a race they are prejudiced against, but rather a gender they cannot control.

Men who are verbally abusive aren't necessarily physically abusive, but, as I noted previously, verbal abuse precedes and is part of all physically abusive relationships. This is a fact the world over, a fact that becomes terrifying in locales where the verbally abusive man is without constraints, where his rage can be fully unleashed. The verbally abusive man may confabulate a reason for his rage that actually defines his partner's or other woman's future—something no one can know. He may then become enraged at what he has made up about her. Consider the extreme case in Multan, Pakistan, in December 2005, where a man slit the throats of his stepdaughter and three daughters, ages eight, seven, and three. Like many abusers, he pretended to predict the future. He said that he killed his younger children because they might do what their older stepsister had done.[14] The admitted murderer claimed his stepdaughter had been with another man, even though all reports were that she had left an abusive husband. This happened in a conservative place where, according to an Associated Press report, "Hundreds of girls and women are murdered by male relatives each year."

The murderer called it an "honor killing." I would say that a murderer who commits what he calls an "honor killing" feels dishonored if a female member of his family is not owned, body, mind, and soul by a male. He owns his wife. He owns his daughters, and he owns a female through the man he "gives" her to. He defines women as receptacles for men's unlived selves, not people. And he would rather see them dead than not have total control over them. It is his "honor" to protect this cowardly way of keeping bodies for men's unlived selves so they never have to become functional and integrated people, but can remain psychologically severed from their inner world, their inner selves. Clearly, they define women as if they themselves were women—knew what they were, what they felt, and what they could do.

WOMEN SEEK CHANGE

Women, of course, want to see the verbally abusive man change. I am in no way suggesting that the men I describe in my books would do anything at all like murdering and beheading—though I do know of women whose former husbands and boyfriends were convicted for stalking or attempting to murder them, or in some cases actually murdering them. I am, however, saying that the verbally abusive man serves not only himself and his family but also humanity if he sees what he is doing and makes every effort to change.

To this end, the partner presents the Agreement to her mate. But how does he respond if he won't agree to it? Let's meet the man who will not accept the Agreement, even when he has the opportunity to add to it so it is satisfactory both to him and to his partner. While many men wake up to what they are doing when the see the Agreement and agree to try to abide by it, some don't. Let's explore some of the responses typical to a verbally abusive man who rejects a mutual Agreement.

1. He says, "I'm glad to see that you agree not to do these things."

He then walks away, ignoring the fact that he has seen an Agreement with all the examples being exactly what he has said to his partner. He is pretending that she says these things to him. She can respond with, "Right, I won't do these things. How about you? Will you get back to me in X days (being specific about the date and time), and I will e-mail this to you so you can put in any changes that you want? Then I hope we come to an agreement and can both initial this. Here is the hard copy and here is the tape."

One woman, who heard her husband say what the man in the above example said, managed to have him served with divorce papers two days later. She was so shocked that he would imply that she was abusive and had said all the things she'd heard him say to her, she didn't even like him anymore.

If you choose to stay for a time, for any reason at all, that is your business and no one can tell you what to do. Some examples of why the partner may stay are: She is not traumatized and needs time to make and implement a plan. She leads a busy life away from the abuser most of the time and doesn't feel that she is under too much stress. She has young children and wants to try to live with the abuser until the kids are older. She wants to try again later to see if there is anything else she can do.

If you are the partner of a verbal abuser and choose to stay in your relationship for a time, I suggest that you try carrying a voice-activated digital recorder that your spouse knows about. This is useful if you are with an overt abuser. But check with an attorney first and tell him or her about this plan, as every state has different laws regarding recording.

Voice-activated digital recorders start recording when someone speaks. Keeping it on (outside of the bedroom) may help you to maintain your sanity. If he tells you he didn't say what you heard him say, you will have a record and you will know what was said, and what you heard. I suggest tying it to your belt loop, or sewing it into a pocket, or in some other way securing it.

What will be the outcome of using a recorder? He won't talk anymore, and you can at least live your life as if he wasn't there; he will stop being verbally abusive and just talk like a normal person; you will have a record of his abuse; or he will try to take the recorder away from you. Always carry a cell phone with you in case of a physical assault so you can dial 911.

If you have a record of his abuse, besides knowing that you did hear what you heard, there are other things you can do with the recording. You can upload the conversation to your computer and edit it so you will have a complete and succinct record of the craziness and then use it in many ways. Only you can decide. You may want to give him a copy, so he knows you know what he says. You may want to give it to an attorney. You may want to send copies to family and friends. You may want to send it to a radio talk show. You may want to do an intervention with everyone you know invited over for an open house and a surprise pre-release. You may only want to think about these things so you don't feel so beaten down and helpless, which is understandable.

If you are with a covert abuser, who just doesn't talk to you (except to counter you), doesn't answer your questions, or doesn't do what he promises to do, it is as if you are a single person. He doesn't relate to you and consequently there is no relationship.

2. He takes the Agreement and says, "I'll get back to you."

But, he decides not to show up for the next meeting, or e-mail his partner with changes, or show any sign that he will agree to the Agreement. When she asks him again, he stalls for time. If this were the case, the partner of a verbally abusive man would do well to make a plan about her future and what she wants in it. I suggest that the partner ask herself, "Where will I be in one year or five years?" And, if she has children, "How will it work for them?" if she decides she may eventually leave. Whether she makes a one-year plan or a five-year plan, it will be helpful to her to get the support she needs to put it into action.

No one but the partner can decide whether she will go or stay in the "relationship." If there are no children, then she might ask herself why she is there and whether the stress of being defined—that is, whether having her reality negated and her mind assaulted—is worth it. Stress is a killer. Every woman I have ever talked to, and there are many thousands, says that verbal abuse is worse than physical.

3. Upon receiving the Agreement, he says, "Now you're saying I'm an awful person."

Or he angrily states, "You think I don't know what you're doing." In this way he is defining his partner, telling her what she is doing or what she thinks.

Her goal is to wake him up, not to defend herself against nonsense. After all, there is no place in the Agreement that says what he is telling her. She has not said, "You're an awful person," nor has she said, "You don't know what you're doing." He doesn't know what she thinks. So, she begins with "What?" and might then move on to say, "Where does it say that in here?" while she looks over the Agreement. Or, "Please don't pretend to be me, telling me what I think. Please meet with me on X date, at the same time, and I'll e-mail this to you before then in case you want to add anything."

4. Upon receiving the Agreement, he tears it up or throws his copy in the trash.

If you are the partner of this type verbal abuser, I suggest two things.

1. Save your copy of the Agreement in case you need it to show an attorney, family member, and/or counselor.
2. Save it also so that you can modify it slightly to use as a statement as to why you left, if you chose to do so.

5. Upon receiving the Agreement, he doesn't respond.

He just takes it and when his partner asks him to meet with her to review and sign it, he says he has to check on his schedule at work, or something like that. Then when she asks him the next day he says he forgot, and so on. He is similar to the abuser in scenario number 2, but he starts catching himself when he starts to say something demeaning, and he apologizes when his partner says, "What?" and she can see that he is really trying. Now would be a good time to leave the book *Controlling People* out where he can find it, or if she thinks he might do something she asks him to do, she may ask him to please read it. Or, she may give him this book, instead, and say, "This is where I got the Agreement idea."

The goal here is that he begins to grasp what he does and why he does it. He might want to change very much or he may believe he needs no help and has already changed.

6. Upon receiving the Agreement, he signs it, but he doesn't want to discuss any problems.

He will not admit that he has done anything hurtful. He can't separate his behavior from himself as a person. He thinks that bad behavior means that he is intrinsically a horrible person. He will admit to nothing. Yet even though he won't talk about his behavior, if he is hearing "What?" quite often, he may come to the realization that he needs to do something.

There is no reason why the partner can't present him with an addition to the Agreement, about a month or so after she presents the first one. In the second Agreement, she simply asks him to begin the program outlined in the previous chapter—that he begin the reading, notes, practice conversations, etc.

7. Upon presenting the Agreement, the partner asks him, "Will you get back to me on (specific date) to let me know what you choose to do and if you have added anything or want any modifications to the Agreement?"

He may respond with, "Why should I?" This is a diversion from the question, so the partner simply repeats the question, "Will you get back to me on (specific date) to let me know what you choose to do and if you have added anything or want any modifications?"

If he continues to verbally abuse her by telling her what she is doing—"You're trying to control me," or "You're attacking me"—she, again, asks, "Will you get back to me tomorrow on whether you will sign this and if you have anything to add or want any modifications?"

If he will not answer her, the partner will have to decide what she wants to do. She might decide to take a bigger step—for instance, separate from him since he does not seem to take her seriously. She might leave the room and e-mail him, asking for a date to go over any changes he wants and to sign the Agreement; clearly, if he refuses to respond, he is not going to change. She might continue to say "What?" to his abuse and make a plan to leave.

8. Upon receiving the Agreement, he tells her that there is no way he'll sign it.

When she asks him why he even stays with her when he seems to hate her so much, he says, "I stay to make your life a living hell," which he does. He actually says he prays for her to die.

This man is irreparably damaged, incapable of any empathy, and truly makes his partner's life a living hell, just for the fun of it. He manifests a sadistic nature and could be very dangerous. See the last chapter for more information on escaping. His partner will need to get support from a domestic violence agency, online support group, and someone she can trust to share her experience with. She would do well to look everywhere she can for knowledge and support. Telling your partner you wish her dead may, in some states, constitute the assault part of assault and battery and qualify for a restraining order.

9. After seeing the Agreement he says, "What you do triggers my anger and your tears make it worse. We're unhealthy for each other and bring out the worst in each other. I don't need to sign anything."

He defines her as bringing out the worst in him. Since she is real and not a dream woman, her existence provokes him. She is not as empty as a woman who hasn't been allowed an education. She shows up as a separate person. He defines her inner world, saying he likewise brings out the worst in her, a blaming statement that suggests there is some "worst" thing about her.

He gets angry rather than empathetic when she cries. His entire interest is in himself. He doesn't want to change. Possibly, he is popular, maybe even well known in his profession. His perfected persona may be well accepted in the world, and he doesn't want to put forth any effort to change. His whole interest is in himself. He has no emotional attachment to his partner. In this case, making a long- or short-term plan to leave, getting emotional support and grief counseling all would be indicated. If nothing has worked, she might leave this book for him to read.

10. If the partner has presented the Agreement and then meets with her abuser at the appointed time, and he refuses to sign it, she will need to decide what she wants to do and begin a plan.

In the meantime, by responding with "What did you say?" by keeping a tape recorder on, by reporting any physical assault, she may manage okay.

Since the Agreement is possibly a final effort to wake the abuser and to see if he can begin the work to actually have a relationship with his partner, the partner may need to have a plan to leave the abuser if he won't change. See the last chapter for more information on leaving a relationship. Aside from leaving, if he won't agree to sign, then the partner might ask her abuser, "Why would you want to go on pretending to be me—pretending to be a woman, telling me what I am and think?"

Maybe he will think about it.

A woman wrote to me with the following poem after her verbal abuser refused to change. She had many experiences similar to Jill's from the previous chapter. She was told what she was, thought, wanted, was trying to do, etc. Her abuser refused to consider the Agreement.

Now I, Maiden of Peace, Become the Warrior

The Dragon War Lord has sacked the village of my heart, decapitated the heads of my dreams and set them ablaze before my very eyes.

I, a maiden of peace, tried reason, ransom and surrender to abate his rage, all to no avail. In his greed for conquest, his narcissistic ambition, he terrorized my children and me.

He enslaved us to his whim.

Held us hostage in the dragon's lair and we've suffered much, but in that dark and dreadful place I've finally planned the escape.

I delved deeply into the depths of my wounded soul, and in that abyss, almost forgotten, found a golden key.

With this key, I unlock my resolve.

I shall be powerless no more.

Of my hurt and sword I fashion a sword of Truth. Tempered in the forge of grief, this sword cuts both ways—but always in the right direction.

From the shards of my shattered self-esteem I fashion my armor. I bind the pieces together with the sinew of knowledge, compassion, and with rivets of truth.

Blinded no more, I fashion my shield and buckler from the mirror of my very soul.

My soul—immortal and untouchable—shall rise against this petty tyrant and deflect all the slings and arrows he can muster.

The Dragon War Lord has no power over me any longer.

His vile serpent tongue shall be deflected.

His accusations cut off.

His hurtful tirades shall no longer pierce us.

The Maiden of Peace, sheathed in the armor of knowledge and experience, shall indeed prevail.

14

HAS HE CHANGED?

Quite often, a man realizes that he has been verbally abusive and that he must stop the abuse. He has signed the Agreement and has said, "I never realized I did these things. I'll do anything. Just don't leave me," or something similar. But as sincere as he sounds, the partner can't be sure.

It is very important for you to know that change takes time.

It is likewise very important for your mate to know that your healing and your recognition of his change also take time.

Some men who were verbally abusive have changed. They've reached a greater integration and level of awareness. They not only became aware of what they had done but also did everything possible to change their behavior.

Some men, however, believing that they have changed, have convinced their partners of this, when they really haven't changed at all. The good news is that with the knowledge of the dream woman, we can now explain the mystery of how they could be so convinced, and so convincing, that change had occurred, even when it hadn't. Possibly, that knowledge will be the key that opens the door to change.

Before we look at some signs of change, we will solve the mystery of the man who seems to have changed, believes he has changed, convinces his partner that he has changed, but in fact, has not changed at all. Here is how it plays out. We've already explored the dream woman and how the verbally abusive man anchors her in his partner once he feels secure (moves in, marries, or has a child with his partner). When the real woman shows up with a sign of separateness, he feels attacked, and he attacks back.

Conversely, when the partner decides she has had enough, and he knows that she might leave, he will usually withdraw his dream woman from her. If his unconscious could speak, it might say, "This body *might leave me* now. It's no longer a safe harbor for my dream woman." Then, his *behavior* really does change, but that doesn't yet mean that *he* has changed. It only means that with his dream woman withdrawn and now a vision before his eyes, he starts to see his partner through that vision. She seems more than ever to be everything he ever wanted. She seems infinitely desirable, so he is as nice to her as he was when he courted her (of course this doesn't apply if he is the type who looks for a new body for his dream woman). If the partner decides not to leave, or returns to him after having left, he is even more abusive because if his unconscious could speak, it would say, "She chose me now. She is an even safer harbor for my dream woman." Basically, this type of abuser is nice when his partner is leaving and abusive when she returns. Unless he is in intensive therapy and doing all the work required to change and sharing his insights with his partner, he is not changing.

Change actually occurs when the verbally abusive man integrates his unlived self, dissolves his dream woman, and actually becomes aware of the real woman. This change in him encompasses many behavior changes: greater awareness, an ability to speak in a rational and honest way, a willingness to hear his real partner versus his dream woman, and a real capacity to offer heartfelt affirmation to his partner. Instead of defining her and her experience, thereby verbally abusing her, he validates, affirms, and supports his partner's experiences, views, and so forth, even when he doesn't have the same ones.

HAS HE REALLY CHANGED?

How can the partner tell if he has really changed? If she leaves and comes back, will he be worse than ever? Is his good behavior just the "'honeymoon" stage of the cycle of violence, the part where his unconscious says his partner's body might leave him now? Is his niceness the reason the average battered wife goes back five or six times? How can she tell if change is real?

Let's look at some of the signs of change and then at signs he hasn't changed, keeping in mind that your own intuition and sense of safety are the determining factors as to whether you stay or go. It is also important to know that even with change, you may not feel emotionally safe again. Emotional safety comes from knowing that you can trust your mate not to hurt you again. For the relationship to work, you must not only be able to trust your mate, but you must also be able to like and enjoy him. If you have been traumatized, his voice, face, even handwriting can retraumatize you. Verbal abuse creates such extreme emotional pain and mental anguish that even if he does change, you may still have to leave him.

INDICATIONS OF CHANGE

- He seems relaxed and relieved. Some men let go of the need to control enough to appear to actually lighten up.
- He continues to read about verbal abuse and control, along with other books that give him insight and keep him focused. He shows that he has a commitment to learning and to change.
- He sees a therapist to help him process the issues that disconnected him from his own emotional self. He also reports to this therapist, or a mentor, minister, or sponsor, who keeps him on track and who knows that he is reading, journaling, practicing conversations, and so forth.
- He asks engaging questions. They may be as simple as, "How are you?" "How are you feeling?" "How'd that work out for you?"
- He doesn't pressure his partner for sex when she is still on guard and walking on eggshells. He follows her lead in showing affection.
- If he slips up and starts to define his partner, he apologizes and rephrases what he was saying. For example, he says, "I take that back," or "I meant to say . . ."
- His communications are kind, not harsh. For example, he doesn't tell jokes at his partner's expense or criticize her.
- He is willing to talk about what he is learning from therapy, reading, and his own insights into his issues. He says something about what he is learning such as, "I'm reading this book, and this is what I'm getting from it." He should be able to bring it up, and he should be able to talk about it.
- He shares something about himself now and then—he talks about his work, his life, or something he remembers about himself. For example, "I tried out for basketball, even though I knew I wasn't tall enough, but I did it because my dad wanted me to."

- He always responds unless he really could not hear something said to him. For example, he never gives his partner the silent treatment.
- He answers questions about himself, and his replies are appropriate. He might list his plans for the weekend.
- He expresses appropriate understanding or empathy. For example, "I see," or, "That's great."
- He stops himself when he forgets himself and starts to say something unkind or hears his partner say, "What?" That is, he is open to knowing when he may forget himself and revert to unkind behavior.
- He takes care of himself and reduces stress.

The Partner's Job

Although it is a burden she never anticipated, the partner will need to be aware in the present to say, "What?" when she hears anything that bothers her. It is also important that the partner ask for what she wants, rather than think, "If he loves me he'll know what I want right now. Or he'll reach out to me more than he is." Instead she will tell him, for example, "I'd like more hugs, or more time with you. Would you please spend more time with me?"

INDICATIONS THAT HE ISN'T CHANGING

Callers often ask me, "What would be the warning signs that he's not just changing slowly or seeming to be a little better—but that he is not changing at all?" What follows are eight signs that he might not be progressing in his recovery.

1. The verbally abusive man says, "I've changed," but doesn't show positive communication skills or signs of change.

2. The verbally abusive man continues to define his partner and indulges in one or more of the categories of verbal abuse that I outlined in *The Verbally Abusive Relationship*: withholding, countering, discounting, joking abusively, accusing, blaming, judging, criticizing, trivializing, undermining, threatening, name-calling, denying by "forgetting," ordering, denying directly (it didn't happen), and venting anger at her. And when she asks, "What did you say?" or repeats a question, he does not respond to her.

3. The verbally abusive man changes from one category of verbal abuse to another (see number 2). For example, he stops criticizing his partner but starts countering her every expression.

4. The verbally abusive man wants to change but still doesn't get it. One man, whom I'll call Tim, said he truly felt he was working on his relationship, and in a way he truly was, but he just didn't really realize when he was defining his partner. He told me that the following interaction occurred at a counselor's office. No doubt it did. What is interesting is that the counselor didn't get it either. If the counselor had intervened, I'm sure Tim would have been enlightened.

Here is what Tim told me.

"When I say she is overly critical and dramatic, she responds with, 'I disagree.' Now what? I seldom argue with her—she's too good at it. It's moot and I see that early in the session. What do I do? I stuff it way down until I explode, handing her the victim thing on a silver platter."

What he is saying is that when he verbally abuses her by telling her what she is—"critical and dramatic"—and she "disagrees," he is angry. Surely anyone would want to say, "Stop it," or "How dare you tell me what I am, and how I am. You're not me!"

But, to be gentle about it, all she said was, "I disagree."

Of note is the fact that Tim would feel angry that his partner wouldn't agree with how he defined her. He was so used to verbally abusing her, he didn't even apologize. He felt he had a right to argue with her until she accepted his irrational definition of her. But he couldn't argue with her because she was "too good at" arguing. He felt he must stuff his anger and that somehow it was her fault. He seemed to feel that he could do nothing but later explode at her. He saw her as using his explosion for a "victim thing." It was as if, in some way, he seemed to think it was her fault that he exploded at her and that she would use it against him playing "victim."

All of this revealed his deep unawareness. He was so used to defining his partner that he didn't even see that what he said about her was not okay. In fact, it seemed so okay to him that he shared it with me to point out "her issues"—saying that I should use anything about these issues that will help victims of verbal abusers! There is no doubt that some men are, to put it simply, unconsciously verbally abusive. He saw himself as a victim because she didn't agree with him that she was "critical and dramatic."

If he is on his best behavior, sitting in front of a counselor, or writing to someone about what he said, and has even read books about verbal abuse and control, and he still can't see that he was abusive, his changing, if it were possible, would take a very long time.

5. The verbally abusive man is not able to engage his partner, asking, for example, "How are you feeling?" Women who have been married for as many as fifteen or twenty years often say they can't recall *ever* being asked engaging questions by their spouses. Here are some examples of questions that ask the partner about herself: "What would you do if . . . " "What do you think about . . . ?" "What's your favorite . . . ?"

6. The verbally abusive man is irritated when he is asked anything about himself, like "How do you feel about this?" "What are your plans for the weekend?" "Do you want chocolate or vanilla ice cream with this cake?" If the partner's question irritates him, that is a sign that he is not really changing. He still has a dream woman who knows the answers to these questions.

7. The verbally abusive man seems capable of change. He says he won't tell you what you are, what you think, what you mean because he doesn't live within you, and he agrees to stop when he hears "What?" He tries for a while to control himself, and then he explodes, and says, "I can't do this. I'm out of here." Although he was willing to try to change, he wasn't willing to get support and do the work required. He didn't say, "I have a problem and need more support, need to do the reading, need to practice conversations, need more than anything to get into therapy that will help me recover my childhood, especially my relationship with my father."

Clearly, the sign that he was not changing was that he was not doing the work to change: getting therapy, journaling, etc.

8. The verbally abusive man excuses himself, declaring himself completely helpless. For instance, he says, "I can't say anything right, so I won't say anything at all." He is covertly telling his partner that she doesn't *think* he says anything right, ever. He is defining her by inferring that she will judge everything he says as wrong. He was likely covertly in control, countering his partner, saying no to whatever she said. Now he doesn't answer her at all, giving her the silent treatment, defining her as non-existent—all the while, staying in the dream state with his dream woman.

However, the verbally abusive man who involves himself in the process of change and puts forth every effort to become connected within himself—if he never quits on himself, if he practices what he's learned and nurtures himself and all those around him—can honor the life force in all. He can step away from violence, step away from anger, step away from injustice, and step out of his partner and into himself.

SIGNS HE HASN'T CHANGED
- He becomes angry unpredictably.
- He refuses to ask nicely for what he wants.
- He interrogates his partner.
- He stalks his partner.
- He becomes jealous of men whom he imagines his partner likes.
- He tries to isolate his partner from friends and family.
- He believes men should be in charge of women.
- He believes men are more logical than women.
- He believes men are superior to women.
- He believes God has put him in charge of his partner.

MAINTAINING CHANGE

One man told me that only by making change a part of his life, could he stay aware. Another said, "Unless I read a little every day, I can slip back under the spell of my dream woman." Another said, "If I remember to create a context in which I can stay changed—like, she is my friend, she is on my side, I don't know what she is thinking—it helps so much." Still another said, "I always thought I'd like to tape our conversations to show her what she was doing. She is so good at arguing, but, oh God, all she was doing was explaining why she wasn't what I said she was.

Now we tape our special conversation times so we both know what's happening if things get weird."

A couple can develop deeper bonds through intentional communication, as I described in the section on sacred communication times on page 173, but it is important that they tape their conversations so "if things gets weird," they will know why. Their ground rules should include both the Agreement and an understanding that they can interrupt the other with "What?" or "What are you doing?" if they hear themselves defined directly. For example, the abuser might say, "We have to stop trying to win and we have to fix our problem." Here, even though it may seem like he's trying to arrive at a solution, the abuser is actually accusing his partner of trying to win and of having a problem that she needs to fix. Each person may also speak up, interrupting their mate if they hear themselves defined *indirectly* (as nonexistent) because a spouse has made a unilateral decision. For example, "We're done with this conversation."

One man did change by doing the required work. His wife called me to say, "I don't know what you told him, but my husband is actually reminding me when it's time for our special conversations." She was absolutely amazed and thrilled to give me the good news.

15

CHOOSING TO STAY OR GO

IF THE RELATIONSHIP BECOMES ONE of trust and healing, you may choose to stay. Or, you may choose to go for a short time—a night or two if you are hearing angry remarks, being yelled at, or are otherwise abused. This may bring your verbally abusive mate to the realization that when he yells you disappear. He may then get some help and move forward in changing.

On the other hand, you may plan to separate for some months, to file for legal separation, or to divorce. If he won't change, then leaving him and the abuse behind may eventually be necessary. You must, of course, base your decision on your own circumstances and your own feelings. No one can tell another person what to do. You must also decide for yourself, if you choose to leave for good, whether you will give him any warning. Is it safe for you if he knows? Will he physically threaten you or harm you? Will your mutual funds disappear if he has advance warning? Might he be more than verbally abusive?

A woman wrote me the following note; it is truly apropos. "I know that the ultimate question is 'Can an abuser change?' If your book was *my* lightning bolt from God, the lawyer's letter was *his* epiphany. He is taking full responsibility for his actions. He can taste his regret, and is sickened by how much he has hurt me and possibly the children."

Her husband did not take her seriously until she initiated legal action. This is unfortunately true of some men. They don't see their partners as separate people until they are shocked awake by their partners' independent actions. Although this woman's spouse became aware that he had been abusive, he would need to work at changing. Only she can tell if he is doing what is necessary and stopping all forms of abuse, or if he is simply hoping an apology will take care of everything.

As I discussed earlier, but worth recalling here, if a verbally abusive man sees that his partner is leaving, he may appear to change instantly. If you experience this, it may be because he has withdrawn his dream woman from you, and you are no longer a secure harbor for her. Know that if he hasn't really changed and you accept him back, he may feel secure and reanchor his dream woman within you.

STAYING FOR THE RIGHT REASONS

If the partner wants to see whether her mate will change and their relationship will heal, she may still separate from her mate to give herself time to heal and time to see if he does change. As a guideline, it is usually a good idea to decide on the period of time they will be separated, say one to six months. When the period of time is up, she will reassess the relationship. She should also plan to meet with her mate at predetermined times for conversation. Generally, when separated, the partner decides when and how often she will see her mate to determine how their conversations work out and what their encounters reveal to her. In this way, she will better be able to tell if he is changing. If these limits are not decided up front, he may constantly call. Partners often comment on this, like this woman: "Every day my husband is endlessly repeating how we must get back together as a family and is begging and pleading with me to return. He tells me how I must be compassionate. He doesn't realize it's about trauma not compassion."

Whether the partner is staying in the same house or is separated from her spouse for a period of time, she may decide to stay in the relationship, if:

- They have an actual relationship, that is, he sees and hears her
- Her spouse is abiding by their Agreement
- He is doing the work and is telling her what he is learning
- She sees that he has empathy for her
- He apologizes immediately if he slips up and says something unkind
- He is supportive of her life and her interests
- He is responsive and asks nicely for what he wants
- He accepts a "no" from her and does not pressure her for a "yes"
- He respects her thoughts, opinions, choices, even when they are different from his
- She likes and trusts him and can love him

STAYING FOR OTHER REASONS

If the partner does not understand how her mate uses his dream woman, anchored in her to complete himself, she may stay with him thinking that somehow, when some external change (such as a move or new baby) takes place, he will change and be nicer. This can't happen, however, because he has not changed his way of "connecting" to her through his dream woman. There are many false assumptions that can keep the partner in the relationship. She may stay for the wrong reasons if:

- She thinks that his behavior has something to do with her.
- She thinks that it "takes two" and she needs to change herself.
- She thinks that if she changes he will change.
- She believes that her religion demands that she stay.
- She believes that what happened would never happen again because he promised.
- She feels bad for her mate, sad for his unhappiness and the difficulties he is having.
- She believes that he is the same as all men.
- She believes she will be the "bad one" if she ends the relationship.
- She believes no one understands about the horror of verbal abuse.
- She believes that her children are better off seeing her abused than having a single mom.

PREPARING TO GO

If the verbally abusive man sees you and any children you may have together as extensions of himself where he has anchored parts of himself in dream woman/dream child, and if he has perfected a faultless persona or image to the world, he may do everything possible to keep his children and punish you as the "horrible person." He may tell the children that their mother hates them and that is why they are not together. I hear this story from women daily. Thousands upon thousands of men do this and either are unaware or do not mind that they are in the process of destroying their children's emotional well-being.

STAYING WHILE PREPARING TO GO

Some partners choose to stay for a while if:

- They have no job and don't know what they can do.
- They have no outside support and don't know where to get it.
- They fear for their lives.
- They fear his threats to take away their children.
- They fear his threats to break them.

I hope that anyone who ends up in a divorce or permanent separation, would resolve not to mention the ex-spouse (or soon-to-be-ex-spouse) to any children. If one does talk about the other parent in a derogatory way, he or she should not be surprised if the child is damaged and ends up with serious problems. On the other hand, some fathers have accused their wives of alienating the child when the child reported abuses and/or sexual molestation by the father. See "Child Custody and Documentation," page 213.

The verbally abusive man who thinks he does not pretend to be his partner and know what she should do, may think that his partner's leaving is wrong and that she should come back. It may be very hard for him to realize that she is a separate person; or, if he has changed to some degree, it may be difficult for him to accept that she may be too traumatized to stay. If, in fact, he really had changed, he would see her as a separate person and know that he couldn't determine what was best for her. He would do everything to support her in leaving, if that is what she chooses to do, very much like the man I wrote about in *Controlling People*, who understood his partner's trauma and who had empathy for her. He said, "All I can do is support her in her plans. I can't blame her . . ."

BEWARE OF FALSE PERSUASION

No matter how difficult and abusive the relationship was, leaving is usually a huge life-changing event for the partner. And sometimes after the partner leaves the relationship, the verbally abusive man suddenly says he will do anything to bring her back. Below is an example of what a number of verbally abusive men have told, e-mailed, or written to their partners after they have separated. The partner of this man shared it with me.

> "I want more than anything to be with you. I love you so much. I can honestly say I cherish you. I am committed to providing unconditional love to you. I just didn't know how to show my love for you. Having you in my life makes me the luckiest man in the world. You are just so great. I do not want a divorce. I think of you all the time and think of how wonderful you are. You are so smart, so fun, so gentle, such a great person. The best thing I ever did was marry you. I want to give you everything a woman could want. All my memories of you fill me with bliss. We have so much good going for us. We so much want the same things, the same kind of life, and we share the same values. We can have such a wonderfully happy relationship. I can see it. We just never tried enough. Come back and we can have it all now. I know we can.
>
> "I feel that we were meant to be together. Our life together can only get better. The foundation is there and it is solid. Trust me. Now that I have changed and learned so many things, I will never expect you to be different from how you are, which is perfect for me. Now I am calm and relaxed. I've gotten past any issues that held me back. Please give our relationship a chance to flourish.
>
> "I love you now and forever."

It seems that this verbally abusive man was as overt an abuser as he was an overt persuader. Just two weeks before he wrote the above note, however, he met briefly with his partner, and when she said she was not willing to go back to him, he raged at her, shaking his fist in her face, terrifying her so much that she ran from him praying she would never have to face him alone again.

It is no surprise then that the reason she left him in the first place was because he so traumatized her. She said, "He verbally battered me almost daily during the previous two years (and periodically before then)—he gave me the finger in a very threatening way, called me a bitch, told me 'F.U.' at the drop of a hat (I can't even bring myself to use those words), mimicked me, ridiculed me, made light of my career accomplishments, often sneered at me, even blew his top if I gave him the wrong fork etc. etc."

The man we just met, like hundreds upon hundreds of men who send poems, pleas, and praise a hundred times in a third as many days, told his partner of his undying love, of his memories of their togetherness, of how it would be when they got back together, and *never once in a hundred times did he ask her how she was*. How did she feel? Why did she leave? What did she need? Could she imagine ever feeling safe again? What would she need to feel safe? Did she still freeze when she heard his car as he came to pick up their children? Could she ever trust again? What hurt her most when they were together? I ask my clients with similar stories, "Has he asked you about you yet?"

Following is a composite letter that's typical of the kind of request for help I receive on a daily basis. In this sample letter, we see a woman who knows that she doesn't deserve to be treated the way her husband treats her, and she has tried to stop him. Unfortunately, he has only continued to abuse her, and just as unfortunately, he shows some major signs that he is not likely to change. She has not been married ten years. While I encourage some women to seek change by writing up and presenting the Agreement in order to wake up the abuser and to encourage the process of change, this case is a bit different. The abuser is not likely to change, but the Agreement will give him an idea of why she left.

"My husband is very verbally abusive. I try to tell him what is wrong, and he just says it is my fault. I know that explaining doesn't work, but even when I say please don't call me that, in a very calm way, he continues. Or if I say stop it, he blames me like I made him put me down. He says that I should get therapy for my issues and that I'm crazy. He was physically violent a few times in the past, and hasn't been violent lately, but his verbal abuse has gotten worse.

"When I try to get some resolution, so that he will stop and apologize for what he's said, he tells me that he can't stand me. Many times, he says that he hates me. I try to be thoughtful and respectful but being nice just doesn't work. Also, I hate to say this, but I know that he has had affairs so my marriage brings me zero emotional security. What can I do?"

The pattern I see here is that of a man who has a huge dream woman. Or, as one might say, a huge unlived self. This would explain his behavior, though it does not guarantee that it is very predictable, or that there are not other influencing factors. It appears that he is looking for his dream woman in other women—thus, his affairs—while his dream woman is, for the most part, anchored in his wife. Hence, he blames her for his behavior. When she shows up and asks for an apology, he tells her he "hates" her. His wife's existence threatens his connection to reality itself.

Although he is very unlikely to change, I suggest that the partner present the Agreement to him anyway. It will, at the very least, give him a clue as to why she has left, if that is what she must do to avoid abuse. In presenting it to him, she will know that she has tried everything she can to give him an opportunity to come to the realization that he defines her. She suffers much because he tries to shape her into his dream woman through force, manipulation, and threats. When she isn't being his dream woman, he explodes. Having seen the Agreement, he may be less abusive during a divorce if she chooses to get one.

MAKING A PLAN TO LEAVE

If the partner decides to leave, it is essential that she has kept a record of the abuse and—if she was physically abused or her life was threatened—it is vital that she has contacted the police and a domestic violence prevention program.

The partner may leave for many reasons, but the abuse is the prime factor. She may choose to leave if:

- She is afraid of being hurt again
- She is traumatized and retraumatized when she sees him
- He does nothing to dissolve his dream woman—no therapy, no lists, no practice conversations
- He increases the abuse after saying he will try to keep his Agreement

When the partner decides to leave the verbally abusive man, he is often deeply shocked. Even when the partner tries many ways to tell him what is wrong and what she can't accept, even after trying various forms of counseling and seeing the Agreement, some verbally abusive men find it incomprehensible that their partners are leaving them. They attribute the whole break up to hormone problems or outside interference. Why? Because they have not been able to hear their partners. Hearing them would acknowledge real women.

If you are planning to present the Agreement to your mate, you should have a plan so that you will know where you will go if he continues or accelerates his verbal abuse. Possibilities are friends, relatives, a domestic violence shelter, or someone in your church or synagogue. It is important to have a plan to be able to leave the abuse for even a day or two. Ideally, you are able to leave any time your mate yells at you.

I recommend that you know where you would go and that you would feel comfortable going there on a moment's notice. Leaving when abuse starts is often the best thing to do. It is empowering. It is taking action. It is staying safe. And it makes an impact on your abuser. I want to stress that the impact of your going is lessened or reduced to nothing if you tell him where you are going, if you use a credit card for gas or food or anything else that he can check to find out where you are, or if you use a cell phone on his service so he can find out who you call.

If you initiate a legal separation or divorce, you can use the Agreement as a summary statement to advise your attorney of the situation. Your attorney will then know why you are leaving and the type of person you have been dealing with. She or he will be aware that this is a man who will likely play games, use control tactics, hide income and information, and may possibly be dangerous. She or he will see, in just a couple of pages, that you have already attempted to stop the abuse. Your attorney may take extra precautions to see that you are protected and get all relevant documentation. Your attorney will also understand if you seem distraught and fearful. If your attorney handles many divorce cases and sees the summary statement, he or she will most likely know that you may be suffering from trauma and could be retraumatized when you see your mate, and that you might be reluctant to be in the same room with him for discussions or parenting classes. Women who have been in verbally abusive relationships say that the hard part is getting people to believe how bad it was. If you have to exchange a child in joint custody, your attorney may be able to help you set up a safe exchange so that you don't see your abuser. He may get permission from the court to keep a tape recorder on during child exchanges.

You might also take your statement that summarizes the Agreement along with this book to a therapist for extra support so that he or she will understand your distress. It may be clear to the therapist that you are traumatized, or it may not be, especially if he or she was trained to see all relationship problems as a fifty/fifty thing (refer back to Chapter 4). But seeing the Agreement and a book about the problem will help the therapist see how abuse and trauma have affected you.

One man, whom I'll call John, realized too late that his partner had chosen to go, noting how hard it is to go on when a relationship ends. He said that the most important thing, from his point of view, was to listen to your partner. "If men listen," he said, "they will know when something is wrong, long before it is too late."

If a man cannot really hear his partner, she may feel too wounded to stay. That is why it is so important for men who want to change to do the work outlined in Chapter 12, "The Process of Change." Perhaps, if John had asked many engaging questions, he would have heard his partner. Perhaps she did not know how to express what she wanted. Here is what John had to say.

"I grew up with parents who never told me they loved me and showed no affection and a father who was angry about his life. He never talked. My parents never really had any connection, nor did they teach us how to love or be loved.

"I feel so bad for what I did and for never being able to make it up to my wife or show her who I am now. It's easy to say I should be happy for her and her newfound self, and if I really loved her the best way to show her is to let her go. I have not been able to do this. She was my family. She was my children. She was my life. I guess that's not a good thing because look at what it's got me.

"I miss my wife and children more each day and want to be a part of their lives and know I never will. I have not been able to find a place for this and in all honesty I don't know if I ever will. I still see her as part of my life. I see my children as part of her and we should all be together. I can't make her love me and unfortunately, she is doing to me what I did to her, not listening.

"I guess if you hurt someone, no matter what your intent, the trust and desire is gone. There is no time machine so I must live in the reality of what's happened and learn from my mistakes. This loss and this lesson are too much for me to deal with. I realize everything I did and I feel that should be enough for her to forgive and give me a chance, but she will not. Now I need to find the courage to move on and build a new life without my family, or maybe it was all a dream. It was all too real for both of us for so long. I guess you don't have to hit someone to abuse them, or say mean things. You just have to not listen and that's more than enough."

This man spoke from his heart and was in pain as he wrote this to me. I believe his letter will help a lot of people. Of note is that he states that their life together was "too real for both of us for so long," but how does he know how she felt when with him? He wants her to "forgive" him and give him a "chance," but her not coming back is not about forgiveness. It is about her being too traumatized to be with him.

Furthermore, even though he knows listening is important, and that they are divorced, he believes that she is "not listening" when he tells her he is changed and loves her. It is as if he thinks that if she heard him she would agree with him and come back. Who isn't listening? Who is he talking to? Who is he defining?

Create a Checklist

If you are making a plan to leave a verbally abusive man, below is a short checklist that may help.

- Get support. Tell someone about your situation.
- Have your own post office box. Pay cash for it.
- Have your own credit card with statements sent to your P.O. box.

- Have your own separate cell phone service.
- Have your own safety deposit box.
- Keep your journals and documents in a very safe location.
- Talk with an attorney so you will know how to plan for yourself.

I gave the above list to a woman, who later called me to say that her husband closed her P.O. box, found out about the credit card, knew whom she called, knew about her safety deposit box, and tore up her journals and documentation. How did he find them? She paid for the P.O. box with a joint credit card, she put her journals in the drawer in which he would first look, and basically did nothing the way I recommended. Her mistake sadly haunted her for years to come.

No one has to go through this ordeal alone. There is a forum on the VerbalAbuse.com bulletin board where people can post their problems and gain support and information from others who have been in the same situation. There are about 5,500 members and eleven forums, or sections, where one can address specific issues. The bulletin board is private, and there is a number to call to register. To find it, simply go to the site and click on "bulletin board."

CHILD CUSTODY AND DOCUMENTATION

Women planning to leave an abusive marriage or long-term relationship have often asked me, "Can he use the Agreement to gain custody by saying it is what I do?" Custody evaluators don't generally look to see if someone is telling someone that they are too sensitive, jumping to conclusions, stupid, etc. They will look at domestic violence, drug abuse, promiscuity, and failure to get the children to school. But every state and every country is different. Getting advice from a domestic violence prevention group in your area or from an attorney is a good idea.

If custody will be an issue for you and your spouse, it is very important to document abuse in a journal or possibly by recording it—and keep any written documentation in a place where no one would ever be able to find it. If you are not in a no-fault divorce state, custody may depend on what has occurred and how it is substantiated. Always check with an attorney before taking any steps like taping the abuse or publishing what he does on the Internet. It is likewise very important to report any domestic violence and keep a record of that abuse. It is extremely important to take a child to see a doctor if the child has been injured by violence. Your attorney may want to know what went on; your custody evaluator might also.

Even with documentation, however, the judge has the power to decide who will have legal and physical custody of your child or children. The judicial system is not always fair, and there can be huge travesties of justice. With the help of the Internet, we can read what women are actually going through, and we can read the adult children's reports of what happened to them when they were young. These brave young people will eventually make an impact on society. With the aid of the Internet, they won't disappear. As more and more travesties of justice show up, there will be reforms. For Web sites where some of these stories are posted, see Appendix E, page 255.

Paul Jay Fink, M.D., past president of the American Psychiatric Association and current president of the Leadership Council on Child Abuse and Interpersonal Violence, says the council is "more and more concerned with the number of lawyers and judges who know nothing about the kinds of custody outrages that go on when men try to dominate women and to get their children away from them."

He explains, "From time to time, using the Parental Alienation Syndrome or some other junk science that the father's lawyer comes up with, the children are taken away by the judge, and the children, in some cases, have been separated from their mother for years with no opportunity for visitation. It is a disaster."

Dr. Fink notes that the Leadership Council is being contacted more and more by women who are concerned and who have had terrible experiences in the courts. "There are lawyers around the country who know what they are doing and who understand the complexity of divorce conflict and custody battles; and there are judges who are sympathetic to the mother who is being battered and abused by the father—who is richer, smarter, and able to handle things in a more cool and calm way. Often, mothers who are trying to protect their children become hysterical in court and are seen as 'nuts' by the judge and the lawyers, so it makes it very difficult for the women to be successful. The same kind of verbal attack that occurs in the home, and before the divorce takes place, occurs in the court."

It is not uncommon for either parent to utilize a child in trying to gain their ends, so the child often becomes a pawn in the hands of their parents, misused by both of them and misunderstood in terms of their youth, their sensitivity, their lack of clarity, and their cognitive inability to understand what their parents are 'doing' to them. The Leadership Council has been working diligently to try to educate lawyers and judges throughout the country, but," he notes, "it is very complicated because of the enormous power the judges have and of the jurisdictional nature of family courts. Nevertheless, we have to keep working to educate them about what is real in the custody world and why we need to have experts interviewing children, handling children, and, in particular, when physical or sexual abuse is alleged, that the examination of the child be done by experts and that the evidence be allowed into court by judges who often make an assumption that it is a false allegation and will not even let the child or the agency handling the child's problem testify. These are the kinds of problems we are facing."

There are literally thousands and thousands of horror stories shrieking of injustice in the United States. Why? Because some verbal abusers are so extremely controlling that they will do anything to take their child or children away from their former partner because she will not stay and be their dream woman.

Dr. Maureen Therese Hannah, associate professor of Psychology at Siena College, sheds further light on this national tragedy: "In many of these cases, children become worse than chattel; they are weapons. By threatening to take the children away from the protective mother, the abuser inflicts on her the maximum amount of fear and anguish imaginable. The children are the pearls of great price, and so she invests all that she has—all of her financial, emotional, psychological, and social resources—to keep the children with her. In the meantime, the abusive father's tactics are sponsored by the family court system, which has only to gain by colluding with him to turn the children into nothing more than the spoils of this war, which is fraudulently called a "custody battle."[15]

For some reason, and depending on the state, if a child tells a judge of sexual abuse by her father, or if a mother presents the judge with her soon-to-be-ex's convictions for violence (or worse), some judges will give full custody to the abusive parent and take the child away from the protective parent. Most often, this seems to be because the judge is told that the protective parent has told the child what to say. The protective parent is accused of "parental alienation," that is, purposely alienating the child from the other parent.

Knowledge is so important if you are a woman who is leaving. Who will judge your own custody case if your ex follows through on a threat to take your children? What will you do if you are certain he will give you no problem but then he does? If you have children and if you are with a person who indulges in verbal abuse, making your life a living hell so that you know that you will die if you stay, and you decide to leave, please study all the following information, explore the sites and resources in Appendix C, and read everything.

One Mother's True Story of Heartache

What follows is the story of Annette Zender, whose case is unfortunately not an isolated one. She has documented 120 other such travesties. In her own words, she shares how she lost her daughter.

"After finally gathering the strength to leave a violently abusive nine-year relationship, I was served litigation documents in which a contested custody dispute ensued. My daughter's father has a long history of abuse, violence, and domestic violence issues. When domestic violence or high conflict occurs either before or during family law litigation, the Minnesota family courts utilize special services from a county office. Hennipen County Court Services performed an extensive six-month custody study by Dr. Millenacker, who detailed the father's violence and abusive tendencies, recommending safeguards be put in place for the safety of mother and minor child.

"Unhappy with the court services report, my daughter's father petitioned the family court for psychological testing, for me only. This was just a last-minute effort to discredit my character. The psychological testing was administered, and the report, dated January 24, 1997, stated, 'Annette has no psychological problems that would affect her parenting abilities and had no hidden agenda for attacking the father.'

"After the Minnesota trial in 1997, I was awarded sole legal physical custody of my daughter, then age five. Her father was given limited structured visitation with multiple restrictions put in place for her safety: to remain in the care of three doctors and remain on medication; to send signed doctors' releases notifying me if he ceased his court-ordered doctors' care; to not take the child out of the state for three years; to possibly attend group men's anger therapy; to not have guns on his person during visitation; and more. No restrictions were assigned to me. In addition, the Minnesota court granted me a two-year Order of Protection. With permission from the Minnesota court, I moved back to my home state of Illinois.

"The father was not getting his way in a Minnesota family court, so brought additional litigation to Lake County (Illinois), Judge Hall presiding. Equally noteworthy, the father has a net worth of over three million dollars and quickly discovered that justice can be swayed if one has money enough to not only starve out the mother but also obscure the real issues of his own faults by making false allegations against her.

"During the next few years, our daughter disclosed abuse by her father to teachers, the principal, a school counselor, to her friends and their parents. She stated her father was climbing into bed with her at night, sleeping with her on a regular basis, and taking nude baths with her and taking Polaroid pictures of her naked in the tub, physically abusing her on multiple occasions, that he would destroy the house on a daily basis, and that she was frightened of him. The Illinois Department of Children and Family Services investigated the abuse, but it came down to the father's word versus hers.

"In July 1998, Judge Hall rendered a court order noting that the father's 'mental condition' and 'conditional visitation' were put in place for the safety of the minor child. Just prior to his July order, Judge Hall granted an additional Illinois Order of Protection. These additional orders did not discourage the father, so for the next three years he repeatedly filed petitions to change custody. In March 2001, Judge Hall appointed Dr. Daniel DeWitt, a psychological evaluator (aka 604B), and Gary Schlesinger, Guardian Ad Litem (attorney for the minor child).

"On September 11, 2001, Dr. DeWitt and Mr. Schlesinger rendered reports to Judge Hall stating their belief that I made my child fabricate stories of abuse, naming her father as the abuser. Nowhere within their lengthy reports did these men acknowledge the father's abusive history or the statements of a victimized child. Their reports took six months to complete and sported a price tag of approximately $42,000 in fees.

"What happened is every mother's nightmare. Based upon Daniel DeWitt's and Gary Schlesinger's 'opinion,' Judge Hall switched custody to the father. That same day, her father picked her up from school. She was never given the opportunity to return or call home, or to say goodbye to her family and me, and has had no contact with any of us since. Where is the logic? Where is the justice for a scared, abused child? If this happened to me, a mother who had no history of abuse, neglect, and maltreatment issues, it could happen to any mother in the United States of America up against abuse issues, domestic violence, and money."

Years later, Annette wrote the following letter:

"Dec. 13, 2005
"Today is my daughter's 14th birthday. Her name is Alexandra. I have not seen or spoken to my daughter in 1,583 days. On September 11, 2001, I sent Alexandra, along with my 3 foster children, to St. Mary's Catholic School. If I had only known she would not be returning home that day or 1,583 days thereafter.

"This unforeseen upheaval of my daughter's life was a result of opinions by Dr. Daniel DeWitt and Gary Schlesinger that were rendered to a Lake County family court (19th Judicial District, Illinois), Judge Hall presiding. Dr. Dewitt's and Mr. Schlesinger's reports negated the 40-year documented history of abuse and violence issues pertaining to my daughter's father. My daughter courageously came forward after being abused by her father. Dr. DeWitt and Mr. Schlesinger discarded her statements, along with numerous affidavits from teachers and counselors stating the same. Their opinion to Judge Hall was that I made my child fabricate stories of abuse. Dr. Dewitt, Mr. Schlesinger, Judge Hall, and the Lake County 19th Judicial District Court rewarded my daughter's courage by placing her back into the very hands of her abuser.

"I have never been accused of abuse, maltreatment, or neglect to any child and remain an Illinois licensed foster parent. The Illinois Department of Professional Regulation filed charges against Dr. Dewitt in a fourteen-page Amended Complaint with seven counts, on behalf of myself and two other families.

"Today, I have no knowledge of my daughter's whereabouts. Since her removal, she has been moved five times, been in four different schools, has home-schooled herself for the past three years, and has been in the care of approximately twenty-four caregivers that I'm aware of. Her father has the financial wherewithal to afford his justice and continues to run with his victim.

"This is not an isolated incident. This injustice is the Best Kept Dirty Little Secret of the family courts not only in Illinois but also across the United States of America. In our family courtrooms, when a protective parent or the children themselves allege abuse (physical, sexual, emotional, or other) the court-appointed officials and judges ignore the allegations, in what appears to be an institutional bias against women and children who allege abuse."

Since our children are the hope of the world and form the future, we spread the word to bring awareness to everyone that verbal abuse is not okay. It damages children and can affect them for the rest of their lives. It precedes other abuses that further damage our children. To save our children, we must support court reform and justice in the United States. The lives of many children have been turned into nightmares simply because there is no oversight, and there are no regulations, nothing to protect them from the whims and even the corruption that exist in the judicial system.

Epilogue

CHANGE IS ESSENTIAL

Even if you, as the partner of a verbal abuser, are so deeply hurt, traumatized, and exhausted from being with a man who attempts to control you by defining you and your reality that you are quite sure you will soon leave; even if you know that you do not want to see his face, hear his voice, see his handwriting or even his e-mail ever again and are certain no man can change and couldn't care less if one did; even if you can know what it takes for a verbally abusive man to change and what it takes to wake him up to his weird and mind-assaulting behavior, you may, in reading this book, understand the need for change and pass this message on to others. Without people helping others, there would be no change in the world. Hence, change is essential.

Most men who verbally abuse their partners have perfected their personas; they have an affable demeanor and they appear to be the nicest people anyone would want to meet. They fool countless counselors, friends, and colleagues. But they behave very differently with their partners behind closed doors. Sometimes, however, men who verbally abuse their partners are abusive to others, too. They define other people just as they define their partners. Irrational behavior can spread out, so to speak, into the world at large. A man may define his wife or girlfriend: "You're too sensitive"; his child: "You don't listen"; his colleagues: "They only *think* they know what they're doing"; a whole race: "Give them an inch and they'll take a mile"; a whole nation: "They're infidels." Some people have even tried to take over the world by defining others. Hitler is a most obvious example. He defined millions of people as unworthy of life. It is of great benefit to humanity that we recognize when people define other people and do our best to see that they wake up to what they are doing, stop doing it, and thus become rational people. Hence, *change is essential.*

In order to facilitate discussion, we label people by their behavior. In talking of a crime, for instance, the news announcer, if discussing a theft, does not want to have to say, "the person who was accused of having indulged in thievery," when he or she can more easily say "the alleged thief." The long version is too cumbersome. This holds true for many situations and the general public knows that *rapist*, or *alleged rapist*, refers to a person who perpetrated, or is accused of perpetrating, a rape. Labels, like "abuser," are simply short cuts to saying something like, "the person who is indulging in verbal abuse." I am emphasizing this point because, although we may label a person by their behavior (thief, rapist, abuser), it is essential that we understand that *no one lives in another person and knows what they are.* If a person defines someone else's inner world, or very being, saying anything from, "You're creating problems where they don't exist," to "You're a witch," and that abuser wields power or weapons, chaos can erupt and freedom is at risk. Hence, *change is essential.*

People who live in chaos, who hear angry outbursts, or who suffer from the silent treatment, rejection, and hostility in what is, when observed from the outside, a "good relationship," suffer greatly. If they have been told that their pain is their fault, that it "takes two," that there is something wrong with them, they will be more confused than they were already, just from living with a verbally abusive man. Hence, *change is essential.*

If partners of verbal abusers are also told that they should try harder, they may feel suicidal. After all, they have very likely already become exhausted trying to make their abusers understand that they aren't as their abusers define them. If they are told that they were looking for someone who would be controlling, they may spend years trying to find out why they were seeking a type of man that they had no intention of ending up with. Generally, if they are defined in these ways (that is, verbally abused), they may stay in their relationships, trying to find out what they are doing wrong or what is wrong with them, until they become certain that if they stay, they *will* die, physically or spiritually. With this certainty, they may choose to leave, though leaving feels like a "might-die" possibility. Still, they choose to leave rather than surely die. Risking all, facing their future with deep dread, they give up their families, relationships, hopes, dreams, and all they struggled to achieve to avoid the certain destruction of a verbally abusive relationship. The tragic assault to and loss of self, mind, consciousness, and perception, must end. Hence, *change is essential.*

In this way, thousands of relationships end every year. Families break up. Is this the only solution? Maybe not.

Some families may stabilize if the abuse ceases—if change takes place, if the partner is not so traumatized that she can never feel safe with her mate again. If we are to have stable, secure families, and healthy secure children, it is essential that we collectively recognize that those who have experienced verbal abuse over time say it is worse than being hit. It destroys minds and it breaks up families. Hence, change is essential.

Terrorists attempt to terrorize people in many nations, and the world takes a stand against them. But in our homes, hundreds of thousands of women who regularly face angry, raging men or cold, manipulative, scary men are also terrorized—and they are alone. No one sees it, and no one takes a stand against these assaults. These are not physical blows; they are assaults against mind, consciousness, and soul. Any attempt to erase the mind of another is an assault upon freedom. If the verbal abuser can annihilate his partner's mind, replace her thoughts with his so that she says, "Oh, I *am* stupid, too sensitive, trying to start a fight, doing everything wrong," then her freedom is in jeopardy. Freedom, the right to choose, is thwarted, dissolving in confusion and fear. The verbal abuser and the terrorist both have taken a stand against freedom. Hence, *change is essential.*

It may seem that no one could really be terrorized by verbal abuse. One might ask, "If a person isn't hit, how can they be feeling terror? How is their freedom assaulted?" Whether overt or covert, verbal abuse is as damaging as physical violence because it opposes human consciousness itself. For instance, a man may counter everything his partner says, and then tell her that there is something wrong with her when she asks him to stop countering. He may even tell her that he didn't say what she heard him clearly say. He has been defining her. Eventually, maintaining a sense of herself becomes exhausting, and her immune system becomes compromised. She realizes that she is getting sick. She is worn out. She experiences emotional pain each time he defines her. And each time, her abuser can't really see or hear her. At a deeper level, some part of her experiences the reality that when he is closed off from her, the relationship is ended. But no one comes to mourn with her. No one supports her. Then suddenly he is open to her again, asking her something, perhaps, "Is dinner ready?" The relationship, which is an exchange between two living beings, is reconstituted. But later, he again defines her, and she is once again unseen and unheard. The relationship is ended at that moment. Then opened, then ended, and then opened again.

This ongoing assault to her psyche and the ensuing emotional pain and mental anguish begin to be the very things she fears, and soon she is feeling the terror of being tortured this way, one more time. "But wait," she thinks, "maybe if I say or do something different it won't happen." When she realizes she can't make it stop, she is again immersed in fear. And there are often valid reasons she cannot leave, at least for a period of time, and countless times when she believes the lie, "It's all your fault." Minds are truly lost and consciousness assaulted in verbally abusive relationships. Everyone loses in the end: the individuals, the family, the community, and the world. Hence, *change is essential*.

I would like to see that people of all countries and cultures observe that wherever women are most defined and subjugated, and wherever the feminine is most oppressed, chaos reins. In fact, the greater the imbalance between masculine and feminine, that is, the less women and men are accepted as equal in value, and as equal and deserving of freedom with equal rights to determine themselves, there is death, strife, extremism, war, chaos, and terrorism. *Clearly, change is essential*.

Appendix A

VERBALLY ABUSIVE STATEMENTS

THIS APPENDIX INCLUDES AN EXTENSIVE list of phrases that, if said in the relationship, can be incorporated into the Agreement. These words and phrases appear in List 1 and are grouped by how they define a person. For example, they tell you what you are, what you do, what you think, etc. and can be used in Part I of the Agreement. The abusive behaviors appear in List 2 and can also be incorporated into Parts III or IV of the Agreement. Threats appear in List 3, and if you hear them, incorporate them into Part III of the Agreement. List 4, the last list, comprises ways a verbally abusive person may define you by implication. There are many additional ways that the abuser might imply who or what you are, what you do, etc. Any of these are examples that may be the same or similar to ones you've heard.

List 1: Words and Phrases That Define You

He may tell you *what you are*. For example, you're:

a backstabber
a badass ...
a bitch
abusive
aloof
arrogant
an ass
the cause of being hurt—it all goes back to you
a cheater
clueless
a cold-hearted bitch
a coward
crazy
critical
cruel
a cunt
demanding
demeaning
a dirty . . .
dishonest
a dumbass
a dummy
an emotional retard
fat
a fat pig
a fucking . . .
greedy
hard to get along with
high-maintenance
holier than thou

a horrible person
a horrible wife
an idiot
immature
impetuous
impossible
impossible to deal with
incompetent
an ingrate
insane
insensitive
irrational
irresponsible
lazy
a lesbo
a liar
mean
mental
mentally ill
a miss know-it-all
a moron
a motherfucker
a nasty person
a nut case
the one with the problem
out of control
paranoid
pathetic
a piece of shit
a procrastinator
psycho
a quitter
reckless

rude
sanctimonious
sarcastic
a scumbag
self-centered
selfish
self-righteous
sensitive
serious
a slob
a slut
spoiled
stupid
a stupid ass
a terrorist
thin-skinned
thoughtless
a total loser
ugly
ungrateful
unstable
useless
vulgar
white trash
a whore
wrong

He may tell you *what you are doing*. For example, you're:

acting emotional
attacking me
being dramatic

being emotional
bitching
blaming me
blowing it out of proportion
busting my balls
doing it all wrong
doing this to be mean
dumping guilt
feeling sorry for yourself
getting upset about nothing
giving me flack
going on and on
going to any ends to win
jumping to conclusions
just emoting
just waiting for me to . . .
living life through your emotions
looking for a fight
looking for trouble
making a big deal out of nothing
making a mountain out of a molehill
making it up
making me mad
making that up
nagging
not listening
not living up to your potential
not trying
obsessing
overreaching
overreacting
pissing me off

putting me through hell because you're too sick to keep the
    house up
shoving a microscope up my ass
snapping at me
trying to start a fight
watching me
yapping

He may tell you *how you feel*. For example, you:

are afraid someone's going to abandon you
are afraid to learn
are confused
are frustrated
are never happy
are not happy unless you're complaining
are not really committed to this relationship
are not upset
are stressed
aren't afraid
aren't sad
aren't tired
don't care
don't care about anyone
don't feel that way
don't love me
enjoy arguing
feel threatened by my education
feel threatened by my intellect
feel too much
have feelings that are inconsequential
have nothing to cry about

love your parents more than me
only care about yourself

He may tell you *what you need or don't need*. For example, you:

always need something to worry about
don't need so much sleep
don't need to make a big deal out of it
need glasses
need religion to remind you of what you are supposed
     to be
need to go to therapy
need to learn to keep a clean house
need to shape up
need to submit
need to toughen up
need to work on your self-esteem

He may tell you *what you want*. For example, you:

just want to be right
just want to dwell on the negative
just want to have the last word
just want to talk about your health
only want my money
want me gone so you can be with someone else
want to argue
want to destroy my dreams
want to embarrass me
want to hurt me on purpose
want to keep a fight going
want to win

He may tell you *what you don't want*. For example, you:

> don't want that
> don't want a good relationship
> don't want to try

He may tell you *what you are trying to do*. For example, you're trying to:

> accuse me of things
> be right
> control me
> get attention
> have the last word
> make me look bad
> prevent me from expressing my feelings
> show me up
> start a fight
> start something
> win

He may tell you *what you do*. For example, you:

> always make me the bad cop
> always talk about me
> always think I am wrong
> always turn things around on me
> bitch all day
> blame me for everything
> bring me down
> burn everything you cook
> can't follow through on anything

consider everyone's opinion but mine
determine reality
do nothing
do nothing for me
don't pay attention
don't work as hard as me
embarrass me
expect me to be a saint and put up with you
find something wrong with everything
give me shit
insist on fighting me all the time
interrupt me
just won't let things go
nitpick
look for problems
make me angry
make me want to hit you
make me want to hurt you
make no sense
never finish anything
never stick to anything
obsess over everything
push my buttons
read pop psychology books and latch on to whatever little
    fad appeals to you at the moment
read things into my words
see everything in the worst possible light
see the world with blinders on
sleep too much
take everything out of context
thrive on controversy
turn everything into an argument

twist my words around
twist the situation around
won't let me talk

He may tell you *how you are*. For example:

Something is wrong with you.
The problem with you is . . .
You're not sick.
You're not tired.
You've got your head up your ass.
You've never had an original idea.

He may tell you *what you think*. For example, you think:

everyone's judging you
I am wrong
I don't know what you're up to
it is all my fault
I'm going to screw up
people like you better than me
you can get away with anything
you can get away with telling me to stop
you know best
you know it all
you know it all because you read books
you're always right
you're better than everyone else
you're an expert
you're so smart

He may tell you *what you know, should know, or don't know*. For example, you:

> don't know any better because your family was screwed up
> don't know how good you have it
> don't know how to communicate
> don't know what you're talking about
> don't understand anything
> don't know anything
> don't know how to do research
> don't know how to take a joke
> don't know how to talk
> don't know what real work is
> don't know what feeling bad really means
> don't know what it's like to work hard
> know how I felt
> know what I meant
> should know how I feel
> I know you better than you know yourself.

He may tell you *what you should/must do*. For example:

> Clean the fucking house.
> Do my laundry.
> Don't come home until your head is screwed on straight.
> Fix yourself.
> Buck up.
> Get in here.
> Get off my back.
> Get over it.

Get the fuck out.
Go take some Prozac and call me in the morning.
Go to bed.
Go to hell.
Go to the doctor and get some hormones.
Grow up.
Make me some . . .
Pick this shit up.
Quit yakking.
See a shrink.
Shut up.
Shut your pie hole.
Stop getting so defensive.
Submit to me.
Suck it up.
Forget it.
Never mind.
What you're going to have to do is . . .
Do what you're told.
Do what I tell you to do.
Don't *ever* tell me no.
You should do it this way.
You should have known better.
You should have done it this way.

He may tell you *what you did*. For example, you:

did nothing about it
did nothing around here
did it all wrong
did it on purpose

voted for . . . to spite me
poisoned the kids against me

He may tell you *what you can't or couldn't do.* For example, you:

can't cook worth shit
can't control yourself
can't do anything right
can't even keep track of the simplest thing
couldn't get a college degree if you wanted to

He may tell you *your future.* For example:

If you had an education, you'd be dangerous.
No one will love you as much as I do.
You will screw it up.
You would be a terrible mother.
You would always try to be nice—especially if it's a boy so
    you would have him be a little faggot.
You won't understand.
You're going to say . . .

He may tell you *your past.* For example, you:

always intended to leave
always wanted control of this relationship

He may tell you that *you are responsible.* For example:

It's your fault if you're hurt.
It's all your fault.
It was really your responsibility to make me stop what I
    was doing.

He may tell you *how you take things*. For example, you:

> take things all wrong
> take things too seriously
> take me granted
> take everything wrong
> take things too personally
> take things too far

He may tell you *how you act*. For example, you act like:

> a blithering idiot
> a child
> a fool
> a retard
> a loser
> a whore

He may tell you *what you get*. For example, you:

> always get what you want
> always get your way
> get what you deserve

He may tell you *what you have*. For example, you have:

> anger management problems
> bad taste
> a brain like a sieve
> a defect in your personality
> everything a woman could want
> issues

no direction
passion
poor self-esteem
a problem
to have the last word

He may tell you *what you don't have*. For example, you don't have:

anything to complain about
an original idea ever
a sense of humor

He may tell you *what you don't do*. For example, you don't:

make love enough
take care of me

He may tell you *what you are like*. For example, you are like:

a child
a crazy person
an infant
a snake in the grass
your mother
your father
my mother
my father
a pit bull when you hold onto the past
a vulture waiting for me to make a wrong move just so that
     you can pounce on me
a five-year-old

He may tell you that *your perception is wrong*. For example:

> It wasn't that way.
> It didn't happen.
> It's not so.
> It is just your perception.
> It is just your imagination.
> You're wrong.

He may tell you *how other people feel about you*. For example:

> Nobody likes you.
> They can't stand you.
> They don't like you.
> You have everybody fooled.
> They only invite you because they like me.
> They only act like your friends to use you.
> They're out to get you.
> They only like you because you buy them gifts.

He may try to *justify his behavior*. For example:

> If what I say hurts you then it must be true.

He may tell you that it *isn't possible for him to talk kindly*. For example:

> Just write a script and I'll tell you what you want to hear.

He may be *purely evil*. For example:

> He is a policeman in a small town and he says, "I stay to make your life a living hell. And if you go I'll get the kids."

List 2: Other Abuses and Violence

Both parties agree that neither will:

block the other person's door
bump and back up into the other
criticize the other
curse at the other
demonstrate violence
direct the other
drive aggressively
get in the other's face
give the other the silent treatment
grab the other
hit the other
interfere with the other's sleep
interrogate the other
jab the other with a sharp object
lecture the other
mimic the other
mock the other
pinch the other
pound and break things
pour water on the other
push the other down
rage at the other
restrain the other
roll eyes at the other
shove the other
slam doors
slap the other
spit on the other
strangle the other
take away the phone

taunt the other

threaten the other

throw the other across the room

throw the other to the floor

throw things at or near the other

tickle the other beyond limits

wake the other up at night

List 3: Threats

Both parties agree that neither will threaten the other person's life, well-being, or security by telling the other:

I'll smash your face.

I'll kill you.

I'll kick you out.

I'll cut you off financially.

I'll leave you with nothing.

I'm leaving you.

I'm going to take the children.

I'm going to make your life a living hell.

List 4: Implying and Insinuating

Both parties agree that neither will define the other by implication or insinuation. For example:

You didn't think: "What *were* you thinking?"

You don't work: "What did you do all day? *I* work for a living!"

You are trying to start a fight: "Why is everything always a fight?"

You don't cooperate: "When are you going to do *your* part in this marriage?"

You aren't capable: "If you can't handle this, do I need to step in and do your job too?"

You are undependable: "I can never count on you...who knows if you'll do what you say?"

You break agreements: "*I* do what *I* say I'll do."

You are oriented to reality: "Let's get down to reality and out of La La Land."

You should be happier: "Other women would give anything to have your life."

You should accept rough sex: "Girls like that."

You didn't turn out to be what he wanted: "Yes, she's my wife. Be careful what you pray for. You might get it."

You are an object to be rid of: "You can have her/him."

You are unreliable: "Who knows where she/he is?" to all who ask.

You are never good enough at what you do: "I would have done it differently," or, "If it were up to me, I would have . . ."

You can't do what you want: "You don't have time for that! You already have too much to do."

You don't contribute: "I do my part earning the money and all you have to do is spend it."

You're responsible for all lost items: "This is your house. I earn the money, you run the house. You should know where things are."

You tossed it: "Where have you tossed my . . . ?"

You can't be trusted: "I have a trust issue with you [when some detail is forgotten]."

You shouldn't do something: "Why would you want to do *that*?" or, "Why are you *doing* that?"

Appendix B

ALSO BY THE AUTHOR

WHILE WHOLE AND COMPLETE IN itself, this book is also the fifth in a series of books by Patricia Evans on verbal abuse and control; each contains information not found in the others. If you are looking for more information on areas that are only touched upon in this book and you are interested in deepening your understanding of verbal abuse, please review the following so that you will be able to choose which (if not all) will best serve you.

The Verbally Abusive Relationship: How to Recognize It and How to Respond (Adams Media, 1992, 1996)
It is the first literature to identify and describe verbally abusive relationships. It shows what verbal abuse is and gives many examples, defining the twelve main categories of verbal abuse. It also describes the patterns of abuse that show up in these relationships so the reader can better recognize what she is experiencing.

The reader can identify with the emotional pain and mental anguish that verbal abuse creates. Further, the reader can find guidelines on how to talk to any children who might be involved if their parents are separating or divorcing.

Verbal Abuse Survivors Speak Out: On Relationship and Recovery (Adams Media, 1993)
This book reveals other forms of control, such as control of the partner's time and space. It shows how the verbally abusive man ends the relationship when he defines his partner, and it has a chapter on coping while in the relationship. There is also a large section on recovery to help anyone who has been subjected to verbal abuse. Lastly, there are affirmations to give strength to the abuse victim.

Controlling People: How to Recognize. Understand, and Deal with People Who Try to Control You (Adams Media, 2002)
This book presents a new model or paradigm that explains what is "wrong" with verbal abusers; how they use verbal abuse to control their partners; why they don't feel crazy when they tell their partner what they are, think, feel, etc., as if they were the partner and knew the partner's inner world. It also explains what compels them and why they feel attacked by the partner's existence.

Teen Torment: Overcoming Verbal Abuse at Home and at School (Adams Media, 2003)
Here we see how patterns of controlling behaviors crystallize during preteen and teen years. The reader finds ways to educate their own children about verbal abuse, identifying ways of both helping children who have been abused and showing them the hidden fears of those who would define them. Readers who were verbally abused in childhood often gain clarity and recognize what happened to them. This furthers their own recovery.

Appendix C

RESOURCES

Author's site: *www.verbalabuse.com*
For additional information about verbal abuse. Links on the home page direct you to a FOX News film on verbal abuse; a feature on Oprah's Web site where Patricia Evans is interviewed about verbal abuse; an audio interview with Patricia Evans on control and verbal abuse; articles about verbal abuse, domestic violence, therapy, and much more. Finally, a bulletin offers support to thousands of members working toward recovery.

American Bar Association Commission on Domestic Violence: *www.abanet.org/domviol/home.html*
Focuses exclusively on improving the legal response to victims of domestic violence, sexual assault, and stalking. Its mission is to increase access to justice for victims of these crimes by mobilizing the legal profession.

Battered Women's Justice Project (BWJP): *www.bwjp.org*
Promotes systemic change within community organizations and
governmental agencies engaged in the civil and criminal justice
response to domestic violence. While BWJP does not provide
direct legal representation, it provides information on best practices and policies to battered women, advocates, legal and justice
system personnel, policymakers, and others engaged in the justice response to domestic violence.

National Council of Juvenile and Family Court Judges
(NCJFCJ): *www.ncjfcj.org*
Comprised of judges dedicated to improve courts and systems
practice and raise awareness of the core issues that touch the lives
of many of our nation's children and families. Training, technical
assistance, and research is provided to help the nation's courts,
judges, and staff in their work.

National Resource Center on Domestic Violence (NRCDV)
and the National Online Resource Center on Violence Against
Women (VAWnet): *www.nrcdv.org* and *www.vawnet.org*
NRCDV provides support to all organizations and individuals
working to end violence in the lives of victims and their children through technical assistance, training, and information on
response to and prevention of domestic violence. VAWnet is a
comprehensive online collection of full-text, searchable elec-
tronic resources on violence against women.

National Sexual Violence Resource Center (NSVRC): *www
.nsvrc.org*
A comprehensive collection and distribution center for information, research, and emerging policy on sexual violence intervention and prevention. It provides an extensive online library and

customized technical assistance, as well as coordinates National Sexual Assault Awareness Month initiatives.

WomensLaw.org: *www.womenslaw.org*
Contains easy-to-understand legal information and resources to women living with or escaping domestic violence.

National Domestic Violence Hotline: 1-800-799-SAFE (7233)
Offers confidential crisis intervention, safety planning, information about domestic violence, and referrals to local service providers.

National Sexual Assault Hotline: 1-800-656-HOPE (4673)
This nationwide partnership of more than 1,100 local rape treatment hotlines provides victims of sexual assault with free, confidential services around the clock.

National Center for Missing and Exploited Children: 1-800-THE-LOST (843-5678)
Families can call this center to report a missing child and request assistance in their search. The public also may call the hotline to report child-sexual exploitation or a sighting of a missing child.

National Runaway Switchboard: 1-800-RUNAWAY (786-2929)
Gives help and hope to youth and their families by providing confidential crisis intervention and local and national referrals through a twenty-four-hour hotline.

Legal Resource Center on Violence Against Women: 1-800-556-4053
May be able to help you find a lawyer for the civil case if you have a custody case involving more than one state, tribe, or U.S. territory.

Visit *www.nnedv.org* for contact information on your state domestic violence coalition.

Visit *www.nsvrc.org* for contact information on your state sexual assault coalition.

Appendix D

RECOMMENDED READING

IN ADDITION TO THE BOOKS listed in Appendix B the following books may provide additional background.

Emotional Intelligence: Why It Can Matter More Than IQ by Daniel Goleman, New York, NY, Bantam (1995) (1997).

From Madness to Mutiny: Why Mothers Are Running from the Family Courts—And What Can Be Done about It by Amy Neustein and Michael Lesher; foreword by Raoul Felder, Boston, MA, Northeastern University Press, paperback release February 2006. A must-read for those with custody issues.

The Gift of Fear: And Other Survival Signals That Protect Us from Violence by Gavin DeBecker, New York, NY, Dell with reprint by Little, Brown and Company (1997).

Keeping the Faith: Guidance for Christian Women Facing Abuse by Marie M. Fortune, New York, NY, Harper Collins, (1987). This book has a Christian perspective.

Angry Men and the Women Who Love Them: Breaking the Cycle of Physical and Emotional Abuse by Paul Hegstrom , Kansas City, KS, Beacon Hill Press (2004). This book has a Christian perspective.

Dangerous Marriage: Breaking the Cycle of Domestic Violence by S. Rutherford McDill and Linda McDill, Spire (1998). This book has a Christian perspective.

Appendix E

WEB SITES FOR CUSTODY INFORMATION

www.courageouskids.net
Click on 'Stories.' Here you will read what children have to say about their victimization. I think it will amaze you that, as with many institutions, money and influence can defeat justice.

www.leadershipcouncil.org
Offers a wealth of articles and information on custody issues, presented by a nonprofit independent scientific organization composed of respected scientists, clinicians, educators, legal scholars, and public policy analysts.

www.icfcr.org
Here you will see the whole story of Annette Zender's great loss, as well as that of other victims of the system.

www.smalljustice.com

This site serves as a resource for anyone who is facing custody issues. It is a good first stop in exploring the family court system and how custody is determined—often to the detriment of the child.

www.jfcadvocacy.org

Justice for Children is a national nonprofit organization of citizens concerned about children's rights and their protection from abuse.

www.rightsforchildren.org

The Council for Human Rights of Children is an international think tank with a purpose of developing and codifying methods to assure the rights of children are maintained and championed.

READER SURVEY

I INVITE YOU, THE READER, to answer the survey on pages 258–260 so that we might know more about changes in relationships when the partner presents the Agreement.

Your participation in this survey will be of great value and is greatly appreciated. You do not in any way need to reveal your identity.

Please check the applicable responses, and add any additional notes you feel are appropriate. Send to:

Patricia Evans
P.O. Box 589
Alamo, CA 94507

Or send a letter to: EvansBooks@aol.com

I thank you in advance. For more information, visit my Web site, *www.verbalabuse.com*.

I am:

☐ female   ☐ male

☐ single   ☐ married

☐ My relationship is *heterosexual.*

☐ My relationship *is alternative.*

I am _____ years old.

I used the Agreement:

☐ Yes   ☐ No

My mate agreed to the Agreement.

☐ Yes   ☐ No

☐ My mate agreed but did not keep the Agreement.

☐ My mate agreed and kept the Agreement.

The Agreement seemed to help my mate to understand what he was doing and what I wanted.

☐ Yes   ☐ No   ☐ Unsure

He was angry after hearing the Agreement.

☐ Yes   ☐ No

After my mate heard the Agreement,

☐ a. The abuse lessened.

☐ b. The abuse escalated.

After my mate heard the Agreement I have more hope for change.

☐ Yes   ☐ No

I was able to decide to stay or go.

☐ Yes   ☐ No

☐ I am still thinking about it.

This book helped me to understand more about verbal abuse.

☐ Yes   ☐ No

My mate read the chapter "The Process of Change" and

☐ he is working to change.

☐ he is not working to change at all.

☐ he is showing signs of change.

☐ he started to work at change but quit.

☐ he is a lot better than he used to be.

☐ he is worse than ever.

☐ he seemed to change but it only lasted a little while.

☐ he continued to read something about verbal abuse and control daily.

I most want to know:

_____

_____

_____

_____

_____

_____

The most helpful thing about this book was:

_____

_____

_____

_____

_____

_____

ENDNOTES

1. For the male reader who has come to the realization that he has indulged in verbally abusive and controlling behaviors and consequently put his relationship in jeopardy, or for the man who has been forced to respond to his partner in dramatically abusive, sarcastic, or silent and angry ways, this book will give him some tools that can substitute for these unkind responses. It will also help him to understand why he has indulged in these verbally abusive behaviors.

2. *www.crimelibrary.com/notorious_murders/famous/simpson/people_5.html.* According to her therapist, Dr. Susan Forward, "Nicole was battered incessantly, regularly, all the time. I'm not saying 24 hours a day, but the incidents of battery were extraordinarily high."

3. Confabulations allow us to feel sane when we wouldn't otherwise. *Confabulations seem like actual memory* and seem to be the truth to the person who forms or confabulates them. The psychiatric diagnostic manual describes this as an "Amnesiac disorder not otherwise specified. It is evidenced by the recital of imaginary events to fill in gaps in memory."

4. *Kirchberg v. Feenstra,* 450 U.S. 455, 459–60 (1981).

5. A March 25, 2005, news release by the United States Department of Labor, Bureau of Labor Statistics, states: Of the 2.8 million youth who graduated from high school between October 2003 and October 2004, 1.8 million (66.7 percent) were attending college in October 2004. . . . The enrollment rate of young women, 71.6 percent, continued to exceed that of young men, 61.4 percent. For more information, go to their Web site: *www.bls.gov/news.release/hsgec.nr0.htm*
6. *Taylor v. Louisiana*, 419 U.S. 522 (1975).
7. Title VII of the Civil Rights Act bars discrimination in employment on the basis of race and sex. At the same time it establishes the Equal Employment Opportunity Commission (EEOC) to investigate complaints and impose penalties.
8. AFL-CIO published the following: In 2004, women were paid 76 cents for every dollar men received in the United States. For a state-by-state fact sheet go to. *www.afl-cio .org/issues/jobseconomy/women/equalpay/*.
9. See appendix of recommended books; and to fully understand his behavior he would do best to read the following books in this order:

    Controlling People to see why he has indulged in verbal abuse toward his partner, but not toward his colleagues or neighbors, and why and how he has created a dream woman.

    Verbal Abuse Survivors Speak Out to understand both the impact of his behavior and the other forms of control in which he may have indulged.

    The Verbally Abusive Relationship to understand what verbal abuse actually is.
10. *For Your Own Good: Hidden Cruelty in Child-Rearing and the Roots of Violence* by Alice Miller. Translated by Hildegard and Hunter Hannum. Published by Farrar, Straus, Giroux, New York (1990)

11. EMDR therapist information can be found at *www .emdrnetwork.org.*

12. *USA TODAY.* "Afghan teacher beheaded, officials say." January 4, 2006.

13. Another report by SA, April 1, 2006.

14. *www.cnn.com/2005/WORLD/asiapcf/12/28/pakistan.honor .ap/.* Thursday, December 29, 2005.

15. From a report: "In the Wrong Hands™," submitted by the Illinois Coalition for Family Court Reform to the Illinois Attorney General, Lisa Madigan. February 10, 2006.

INDEX

Other Books by Patricia Evans

As featured on *Oprah*!

"A groundbreaking book . . ."
—*Newsweek*

Trade Paperback, $14.95
ISBN: 1-55850-582-2

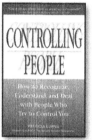

Trade Paperback, $14.95
ISBN: 1-58062-569-X

"[A] timely . . . compelling work."
—*Library Journal*

Trade Paperback, $14.95
ISBN: 1-55850-304-8